BON

WITH YC

In loving memory of Zeke (11/11/98–10/13/08)

BONDING
WITH YOUR DOG

A Trainer's Secrets for Building
a Better Relationship

VICTORIA SCHADE

Wiley Publishing, Inc.

Dedicated to the dogs I've loved and lost: Sasha, for awakening the trainer within me; Ollie, for showing me how easy it can be; and Zeke, for shaping me into the trainer I am today

This book is printed on acid-free paper.

Copyright © 2009 by Victoria Schade. All rights reserved.

Howell Book House

Published by Wiley Publishing, Inc., Hoboken, New Jersey

For general information on our other products and services or to obtain technical support please contact our Customer Care Department within the U.S. at (877) 762-2974, outside the U.S. at (317) 572-3993 or fax (317) 572-4002.

Wiley also publishes its books in a variety of electronic formats. Some content that appears in print may not be available in electronic books. For more information about Wiley products, please visit our web site at www.wiley.com.

Library of Congress Cataloging-in-Publication Data:
Schade, Victoria.
Bonding with your dog: a trainer's secrets for building a better relationship / Victoria Schade.
     p. cm.
  Includes index.
  ISBN 13: 978-0-470-40915-2
  ISBN 10: 0-470-40915-0
  1. Dogs—Psychology. 2. Dogs—Effect of human beings on. 3. Dogs—Training. I. Title.
  SF433.S33 2009
  636.7—dc22   2008054162

Printed in the United States of America

10 9 8 7 6 5 4 3 2

Book production by Wiley Publishing, Inc. Composition Services

ACKNOWLEDGMENTS

I agonized over these acknowledgments for weeks. Stared at the blank page for hours. Started and stopped writing them a few dozen times.

Then I diagnosed myself: gratitude paralysis. There are just too many people who have influenced, inspired, supported, and encouraged me to thank all of them adequately, but I'll try.

To my wonderful clients, both canine and human; my fellow trainers whom I dare to call "peers" (particularly Colleen Pelar and Robin Bennett); the Lunch Bunch; my dear friend Jennifer Buckley, who ran out of exclamation points expressing her approval of an early draft; my editor, Elizabeth Kuball, who curtailed my use of exclamation points; my practically perfect parents; and the rest of my family . . . thank you.

To my husband, Tom, who weathered every writer's-block-induced tirade without flinching, and still wanted to give me a kiss after the storm passed . . . thank you.

And finally, thanks to Zeke and Sumner, who patiently waited for me to stop staring at the computer and put my own advice to good use.

CONTENTS

FOREWORD

What do our dogs really think about us? Consider the bond we have with dogs. They're an altogether different species from our own, yet they share our lives, our living spaces, even our beds—and, most important, dogs share our hearts. Do we share their hearts?

There's no doubt dogs are capable of astounding devotion. What kind of bond do you think Hachiko, an Akita, had with Dr. Eisaburo Ueno? Every day, Hachiko accompanied his master to the train station to see him off to his job as a professor at Tokyo University. Just like clockwork, as if he could check a watch on his paw, Hachiko showed up at the train station at precisely 3 p.m. to greet his owner's arrival. Then, one day (May 31, 1925), Professor Ueno did not return. He had died that day at the university. Hachiko waited and waited at the train station, finally walking home alone around midnight. But he never gave up. The next day, and every day for a decade after, Hachiko went to the train station at 3 p.m. to seek his owner, until Hachiko finally died.

In April 2005, Cindy Hernandez was on TV stations across America talking about Bob, her 80-pound Chow-Lab mix. Cindy was playing with Bob and decided to jump into a pond near her home in Tampa, Florida. She says she heard a loud noise, like a motor boat roaring in her direction; she turned to see a giant alligator's body rising above the water mouth open. Bob came from nowhere and jumped in front of Cindy, giving his life for hers.

Ron Aiello was a U.S. Marine in Vietnam when his partner alerted him to stop and kneel, and to do it now! Aiello immediately heeded the warning. Moments later, a sniper opened fire, just missing Aiello. His partner, who clearly saved Ron's life, was a German Shepherd Dog named Stormy. Ron said he had no idea a sniper was nearby, but clearly Stormy did. Ron says that in the year and a half they were together, Stormy saved his life "a few times." Today, Aiello, president of the nonprofit United States War Dog Association, says, "We conservatively estimate that U.S. military working dogs saved 10,000 lives in Vietnam. That number could easily be as high in Iraq and Afghanistan."

The dramatic and downright incredible stories of dogs so bonded to people that they'll risk their own lives are numerous enough to fill lots and lots of books. Those books have been written. But what exactly *is* this bond, and how do you cultivate it? That topic has not been addressed before, but in this book Victoria Schade does exactly that.

As much as we'd all like to believe the romantic notion that our dogs are so bonded to us that they'd save our lives without thinking twice, it's not likely true. Odds are, most of us will never need to know whether our dogs would give their own lives for ours. Still, day-to-day life with a canine partner is more pleasurable and more intense when the dog is totally bonded. In fact, that totally bonded dog is more than a pet—he's a family member and, in some ways, a partner.

Most dogs are capable of rising to this expectation. Individual dogs have their own feelings, their own opinions about us. For some people, it's a good thing they can't ask their dogs what they really think. That bit about unconditional love isn't necessarily a given—it has to be cultivated.

Our latest addition is Ethel, one of millions of pets adopted as a part of the ongoing Iams Home 4 the Holidays adoption campaign. Ethel was adopted as an 8-week-old puppy from Animal Care and Control and PAWS Chicago. She was—and in some ways, still remains—a challenge. When she was a young pup, she had a condition called pica. More than typical puppy investigative behavior, she sought to eat anything—edible or not. Her energy remains boundless and her attention span and impulse control are much like my own: nonexistent. We had to control her vacuum cleaner appetite to prevent a medical emergency, and dealing with her boisterous (albeit fun-loving) attitude has been challenging. Now, at over 2 years old, Ethel has an intense bond with me. But the notion that these things just happen isn't so. Early on, though I am a certified canine consultant, I sought the advice of various experts, including Victoria Schade. She helped us, and now she can help you. You, your dog, and the relationship you have with one another will benefit from the advice she offers in this book.

Steve Dale, CBC
Host *Steve Dale's Pet World* and *The Pet Minute with Steve Dale* (www.petworldradio.net), *Pet Central* (WGN Radio, Chicago), syndicated newspaper columnist (Tribune Media Services), contributing editor *USA Weekend*
www.stevedalepetworld.com

Part I

ALL ABOUT BONDING

Chapter 1

WHAT IS THE BOND?

Beth threw up her hands and huffed, "This dog hates me."

Hate? Not exactly. Daisy, Beth's dog, hadn't acted the slightest bit angry toward her. In fact, Daisy was sitting placidly at my feet, panting, smiling, and having a grand time practicing sits and downs. I couldn't detect a speck of hate in the Standard Poodle before me. She was a perfectly lovely dog.

But Beth was half-right. Something was off between dog and owner, and it hung in the air like last night's party. It was enough to make Beth downright angry, and me somewhat embarrassed. I tried laughing off Daisy's strange behavior, but Beth wasn't having it. "I feed her, I walk her, I pet her—but she's ignoring me! Why does Daisy like *you* better?!"

Ouch.

Beth had contacted me because Daisy constantly "blew her off" and didn't listen to her. We were in the middle of our second training session of six, and I had to admit that Beth was right. Daisy was excelling at her sit-stays, downs, and recalls—*for me.* And that was the problem. Daisy acted as if Beth weren't even in the room during our lesson.

Beth waved a piece of hot dog in front of her dog's nose, "See! I have them, too!" and asked for a basic sit, only to have Daisy turn her back on Beth and walk over to me.

Every dog trainer has a little bit of Doctor Dolittle in them, no matter how hard we try to avoid anthropomorphizing. I couldn't help but fall prey to it yet again with Daisy. Every time she looked at me, she seemed to be saying, "You understand me. You make sense. *Thank you.*"

I thought a change of venue might make things more pleasant for all of us—the tension was thick inside—so we suited up to go for a walk. Unfortunately, the leash walk was worse. After I convinced Beth to let me walk Daisy without a choke collar—a training tool that I consider outdated and unnecessary—I demonstrated my technique with inspiring results. Daisy was a fabulous walker! She matched her pace to mine and glanced up at me every so often as if to say, "Am I doing this right?" I paid her with tasty treats every few steps to assure her that she was right on track. Once I was confident that Daisy had grasped the basic loose-leash walking concept, I turned the leash over to Beth. "My last trainer told me to keep the leash tight and make sure that Daisy walks at least two steps behind me. Why didn't you mention anything about that?"

"Well," I said, "leash walking should be fun for both of you. Keeping the leash tight and making Daisy walk right beside you turns what could be a pleasant stroll into a military drill. Casual loose-leash walking allows her to sniff the pee-mail and check out the neighborhood goings-on, which is all she really wants to do."

"But my last trainer said. . . ." And the pattern continued while Daisy tripped, pulled, and ignored Beth. I asked for the leash again, and Daisy immediately fell in step near me, looking at me every so often in the hopes of getting a much-deserved hot dog. "Why doesn't she do that for *me?*" Beth asked angrily.

"This is going to be a long six weeks," I thought to myself.

Because I do private lessons in my clients' homes, I'm able to pick up a great deal of background information about the relationship between dog and person before the lessons even begin. I start the training process by doing a quick Q&A with my clients, but I get just as much information from watching the interactions between them during our initial conversation as I do from the interview portion of the meeting. I noticed a problem between Beth and Daisy as soon as I met them, but I never dreamed that Daisy's inattentiveness to Beth would hobble the training process as dramatically as it did. While I was there, the dog wanted nothing to do with Beth. Daisy happily performed each exercise with me, but when it was Beth's turn, Daisy walked away. "Oh, this is *normal!*" I tried to joke, "I'm the Hot Dog Lady. It's not me that she loves—it's what's in my pocket!" However, it was clear to both of us that something wasn't right between dog and guardian. The problem was compounded by the fact that Daisy's snubs absolutely enraged her person. Beth acted like a jilted girlfriend—petulant, jealous, and overbearing—every time Daisy ignored her, which only drove Daisy farther away from her person. It's hard to avoid playing amateur psychiatrist in these situations, and all I could think was, "Issues, issues, issues," as I tried to salvage the lesson.

Beth quit training with me after the third session, and I guiltily admit that I was happy. However, I felt terrible for Daisy, the clever, sweet dog who clearly needed an ally. Sure, I could tell that there was some sort of relationship problem between dog and owner, but aside from offering standard obedience-training advice, I'd done nothing to solve it. The concept of the bond began to percolate in my brain.

The Beth-and-Daisy debacle certainly wasn't the first time I had dealt with a relationship-challenged duo. When I began my training career, I thought relationship problems like inattentiveness were obedience issues. The dog wouldn't come when called and pulled like a sled-dog on leash. Dog-friendly training will save the day, right? Sometimes yes, sometimes no.

When it didn't, it always seemed that something was off between dog and owner. There was a lack of spark between them—but how could I describe *lack of spark* to a frustrated dog owner without sounding like a kook? Most of the time, the owner didn't even realize that there *was* a bond problem. The owner thought she had a disobedient dog—a "bad" dog—but never looked at the relationship with her dog as a two-way street. I struggled to understand why there was no spark in these dicey pairs. How and why did these relationships go off the rails?

Happily, I also work with an equal number of inspirational dog-human pairs. Robert and his Bichon Frise puppy, Cody, really won my heart. I was concerned when I first met Robert, because he was older than my average client, and senior clients who have trained dogs in the past are used to a harsher, more traditional type of training. But Robert took to my dog-friendly methods quickly, and both he and Cody became star students. Each week when I arrived I was treated to "The Cody and Robert Extravaganza," which was basically five minutes of the two of them showing off everything they had practiced during the week. At the third lesson, after Robert had given me Cody's weekly progress update, he smiled and said, "Watch this."

He looked at Cody and said, "Bed!" Cody leapt up, did an about-face in the air, ran down the hall, and disappeared into a room. "No way!" I exclaimed. We traced Cody's steps down the hall and sure enough, there he was, sitting on his dog bed grinning at us. Amazing! I was so impressed by their hard work and joyful collaboration that I welled up with tears. (It happens all the time—I'm a sucker.) By the fifth week, I had nearly run out of things to teach them!

The strength of their relationship was evident in ways other than just their obedience skills. Cody was always happy to see me and willingly worked for me, but he had a regard for Robert that was magical. If Robert lagged behind during leash walks, Cody split his time between walking next to me and stopping and waiting for Robert to catch up. If Robert walked out of the room, Cody perked up and followed him out, even if the Hot Dog Lady was sitting next to him on the floor. There was a chemistry between them that manifested itself in everything they did.

My experiences with clients like Robert and Cody and Beth and Daisy inspired me to try to dissect the specifics of the dog-human relationship, and determine just what the bond is. No small feat. We all know that a bond exists between dogs and people, but the assumption is that it just *happens*. Our dogs love us, and we love them back, right? We fill their food bowls and take them for walks, and they, in turn, worship us for it and obligingly do everything we ask of them.

Not quite.

Beth loved Daisy, and I'm certain that Daisy loved Beth back, but it was clear to all of us that love was not enough. Love was not enough to coax Daisy into *wanting* to work for Beth, despite the fact that Beth had a pocket full of hot dogs. It wasn't enough to make Daisy notice when Beth left the room. And it certainly wasn't enough to keep Beth from getting incredibly frustrated and emotional with her dog. The more I thought about the dog-human bond, the more it became apparent that, while love is at the core, there is much more to it.

While dissecting the bond concept, I thought about my relationship with my dogs, Zeke and Sumner. Although they're far from perfect dog-trainer demo-dogs (in fact, they frequently embarrass me), we do have a pretty inspirational bond. I no longer do formal training with them, but they reliably perform stays in distraction-filled environments. I can leave my lunch on a low coffee table, tell them "Please don't," and leave the room, confident that I'll come back and find the intact sandwich next to a puddle of drool. They actually listen when I ask them to ignore the neighbor's tipped garbage can. They respect the "no dogs allowed" boundaries in our house. And if I accidentally leave the back gate open, they walk right up to the front door and wait to be let back in instead of terrorizing the neighborhood.

I discussed the bond concept with my dog-trainer friends. Why were our dogs *exceptionally* bonded to us, despite our varying commitments to training them? And why did our clients' dogs bond to us so quickly as well?

It became clear that we all unconsciously do a number of things with dogs that enhance our relationships. Some of the skills come to us naturally because we spend our days knee-deep in dogs. Some of the skills are born of necessity, in an effort to keep busy dogs and overwhelmed owners focused on the task at hand. People assume that dog trainers have a magical talent—an ability to "whisper," if you will—that allows us to communicate with dogs in a way not possible for the average dog owner. The public is led to believe that dog trainers are born, not made, and only certain people are blessed with this gift to connect with dogs. Unfortunately, that's a fallacy—one that's currently selling a lot of books full of misleading information. In my quest to define, and later teach, the easiest ways to strengthen the bond with our dogs, it became abundantly clear that *anyone* who wanted to could.

So what exactly is this mystical bond between humans and dogs? How do you know if you've *really* got it? And if you don't "got it," how do you get it?

It's time to take a step back and really look at the relationship you have—or don't have—with your dog. If you find yourself frequently frustrated with, embarrassed by, and agitated with your dog, despite all the training you've done with her, you've got a disconnect that needs to be addressed. In this book, you'll find the six building blocks for creating a positive, mutually rewarding, envy-inducing bond with your dog. My suggestions are like individual sections of a rope that braid together—they're stronger when they're intertwined. The steps are easy to incorporate into your everyday routine, and, most important, they're truly dog friendly. Some are silly, some are unorthodox, but they've all worked for me and legions of my clients—and they'll work for you, too.

Let's get started.

Though tempted, Sumner won't steal the sandwich.

Relationship Quiz: How Strong Is Your Bond?

To gauge the strength of your bond with your dog, ask yourself the following questions:

- **Does your dog check in with you during walks? Does she occasionally look up at you as you walk, or is she at the very end of her leash the entire time?** Many of my clients have what I call "sled-dog walks," where the dog is at the end of the leash, doing everything in her power to move forward with no regard for the person at the other end.

  Granted, there's a major obedience aspect to polite leash walking, but my question dives deeper than just basic manners. Does your dog even know that you're *there,* or are you just deadweight that keeps her from moving forward faster? A dog who keeps her pace similar to yours and *checks in* (looks up at you every so often) is acknowledging your presence and participation in the walk. You're sharing the experience. The distance between you and your dog during a walk should not be based solely on the length of the leash—just because it extends fifteen feet doesn't mean that your dog should be walking fourteen and a half feet away from you.

  A caveat: Fearful or reactive dogs pull while leash walking for reasons unrelated to bonding. Nervous dogs are in fight-or-flight mode, and these types of pullers need behavioral modification to deal with their leash issues.

This dog is on a mission. He seems to have forgotten that his owner is with him on the walk.

This dog is in sync with her owner during their walk. She's keeping a similar pace and is checking in with her owner by looking up at her.

- **Are you afraid that if your dog slipped out the front door unleashed, she'd take off running and not come home?** During my Q&A sessions with new clients, some will laughingly tell me that when they open the front door, their dogs take off without a backward glance, not realizing that this issue paints a rather dismal picture of their relationship. I understand that certain breeds have a genetic predisposition to wander, explore, and chase rapidly retreating objects, but I don't think that those tendencies are the sole reason why some dogs make like escaped convicts every time they get a whiff of freedom. If you're going through complicated rituals to make sure that your dog can't slip past you when the door opens, it's time to revisit basic training and give some thought to just why she doesn't wait to see if you're coming out, too.

- **Do you think your dog is "too stubborn" or "too dumb" to learn basic obedience behaviors?** You probably took a training class with your dog when you brought her home. The first class was fun, the second class was tough, and then you gave up somewhere at the third or fourth week because your dog was the most excitable dog in the room, or the slowest dog in the room, or because you didn't have enough time

"Are you coming with me?"

to get to class, or you just didn't enjoy it as much as you thought you would. And now your dog is saddled with a label that she doesn't deserve.

I've worked with many people who believe that their dogs can't figure out basic obedience training—and it brings me great joy to prove them wrong within minutes.

- **Does your dog seek you out in new environments (for example, at a crowded dog park)?** You show up at your local dog park and, of course, your dog takes off to sniff bums. That's why she's there! But does she circle back to check in with you at some point, or are you as good as a fence post until it's time to go?

In the hierarchy of what's important to dogs, other dogs are right at the top of the list, so it's no surprise that you're invisible when you first arrive at the park. However, you should be more than just your dog's chauffeur and gate opener. The bonded dog wants to know where her person is no matter how intriguing the surroundings.

It can be particularly difficult to get your dog's attention at the dog park.

- **Are you frequently frustrated with your dog?** You're reading this
  book, so it's a safe assumption that your relationship with your dog is
  frustrating you. There's a degree of frustration in every dog-human
  relationship, but the word *frequently* in my question hints at the real
  problem. If frustration, which is only a few steps away from anger,
  forms the foundation of your relationship with your dog, how can there
  be any room left for joyful communication?

Answering yes to just one question wouldn't necessarily trigger a bond
alarm, but the combination of several yes responses suggests that you might
have a tenuous bond with your dog.

My questions were leading on purpose. You're probably more than aware
that you and your dog are not in sync, but the goal of the questionnaire,
though painful, is to shine a light on the heart of the bond issue between you
and your dog. If you answered yes to the majority of these questions, you
don't really matter to your dog when it counts.

There are a myriad reasons why that might be. It's scary to admit, but it
could be due to abuse (which I dearly hope is not the case), or the temperament, age, or breed characteristics of your individual dog. Did you research
your dog's breed before you got her? Are you an apartment dweller trying to
figure out how to live with a high-drive German Shorthaired Pointer? Maybe

you just rescued a dog and you haven't had a chance to build a strong bond. Or maybe you're a first-time dog owner befuddled by too much conflicting advice. Maybe you're too busy working to give your dog the attention she needs. Or, on the flip side, perhaps you've given your dog *too much* freedom and she's convinced that it's *her* world and you're just livin' in it. There are endless possibilities as to why you and your dog don't have the relationship you'd like.

On the surface, it might appear that you have a sound relationship with your dog. After all, she follows you around the house, and leaps deliriously when you come home each day. But there's little competing interest in those scenarios—you're the only game in town!

Introducing the Bonded Dog

So let's take a closer look at the bonded dog. What's she like?

The bonded dog listens to basic obedience cues without thinking—it's natural for her to respond when you ask. Training is a part of her everyday routine, not something you only attempt in special circumstances, so that she'll hold a stay when you ask or come running when you call. The bonded dog wants you in her sightlines, even when she's in intriguing environments. She doesn't head out the door and take off for parts unknown, because there's no better copilot than you—you bring the fun! The bonded dog follows your house rules once you've worked through them with her. Best of all, she thinks that you're the coolest being around—as entertaining as her canine friends, almost as fun as birds and squirrels, and more scrumptious than the three-day-old bagel on the sidewalk. You've seen well-bonded dogs and their people around your neighborhood or at the dog park—they have the relationship you envy.

Now on to the big question. What is the bond? Is it love?

Not exactly. Love between you and your dog should be a given, and this isn't a book to help make your dog *love* you more. (Most people are offended when I suggest that they might have a bond issue with their dog. The first response is usually, "Oh, I know my dog loves me.") There's no question that you love dogs, since you've made the choice to introduce a dog into your home. Why else would you put up with muddy paws, saliva stalactites, fur tumbleweeds, and inquisitive noses? Dogs provide the limitless positive adoration we crave but don't always get in our human relationships.

Most people cite dogs' unconditional love as the reason *why* the love between human and dog is so deep. Dogs adore us despite our extra pounds and occasional moodiness. They forgive us when we ignore them to meet an important work deadline and when we accidentally lose our temper. A dog's love is boundless, and therein lies the reason why she has earned the title "(wo)man's best friend."

Does your dog come running when you call?

The bond is certainly rooted in love, but it's different from love. For example, my client Tina's Chinese Shar-Pei, Benson, adored her. The breed gets bad press for being independent and standoffish, but Benson was a Shar-Pei who actually *liked* to be cuddled and fussed over. I had high hopes for what Tina and Benson would be able to achieve in our sessions. Unfortunately, once we began training, things changed.

Benson simply didn't want to work for Tina. Sit? Maybe, if he felt like it. Come when called? No, thanks—there's good stuff to sniff over here on the kitchen floor. Things only got worse when we moved the training outside. Benson found every blade of grass far more intriguing—and rewarding—than his person. We could easily have written off his less-than-stellar performance on the breed standard: stubborn and aloof. But his performance for me? Awesome. It wasn't that Benson was too stubborn to train, he just wasn't interested in training with *Tina*. I had no doubt that Benson adored her, but there was something missing in their perfect-on-the-surface relationship. Unfortunately, Tina blamed Benson's responsiveness with me on my pocket full of treats. The truth was her loving relationship with Benson, combined with her pocket full of the very same treats, should have easily trumped me.

"Love is all you need." If only. I'd probably be out of a job if that were the case! Of course, you can't have a bond without love, but you certainly *can* have love without a bond. I think both Benson and Daisy loved their owners very much, but it seems conditional: "I love you and will acknowledge you when nothing else is going on. I love you when there are no dogs, birds, squirrels, strangers, chicken bones, mulch chunks, swirling leaves, or errant molecules anywhere in sight."

I hold the potentially unpopular view that the bond between you and your dog is actually *more important* than the love between you. While love develops naturally (one hopes), building a strong bond needs time and attention. It doesn't happen automatically, like love—the bond develops through every interaction you have with your dog, and what you do, say, and even think all play a role in either strengthening or diminishing the bond you have with your dog. The bond forms the core of your entire relationship; if it's lacking, it's the source of the majority of your frustration with your dog. A strong bond is the reason your dog wants to be close to you, work for you, and listen to you.

But what is it *exactly?* Here's how I look at the alchemy of the bond: It's a relationship steeped in love *plus* equal parts mutual respect, trust, and regard. In short, it's the glue of your relationship with your dog. (Sounds like a marriage.) Let's examine the specifics of my definition.

Mutual respect

The concept of mutual respect is bound to ruffle a few feathers, as many trainers believe that respect need only be paid from the dog to the human, not vice versa. Indeed, it's critical that your dog understands that you are keeper and controller of the fun stuff, and worthy of respect. A household lacking canine respect is a household in turmoil.

Take Katie, a college student and owner of Tucker, a *massive* Golden Retriever. Katie adored Tucker, but she never instilled rules or boundaries in her household, so she ended up with a pushy, obnoxious, almost unbearable dog who ran the show. If Tucker saw something on the counter that interested him, he leapt up and helped himself. When he wasn't getting enough attention, he jumped on the closest human and nipped to try to get a reaction. Respect? Tucker gleefully did what he wanted when he wanted, and no one was stopping him. Katie was merely a speed bump on the road to getting his way.

I don't believe that respect should be a one-way street in the canine-human relationship. Showing your dog respect will not upset the natural order of the animal world, nor will it leave you with a dog who is plotting a coup to overthrow the household. Historically, gaining respect from your dog required a heavy hand and a hard heart—you could swap the word *respect* with *fear* and probably end up with the same dog-training to-do list. Looking at respect as a mutual effort, though, softens the hard edges of the concept. Respecting your dog means:

- Treating him as a sentient, feeling being, given to moods and, yes, bad days. (We're quick to forget that dogs aren't little computers to be programmed.)

- Accepting your dog's limitations—maybe your dog doesn't *like* to play fetch, despite what the breed description says.
- Using kindness and patience to train.
- Refraining from physical means to "correct" bad behavior or enforce household rules.

Respecting your dog is almost as important as your dog respecting you.

The love between dog and guardian should happen naturally. Developing a strong bond takes time and attention.

Trust

The second part of my definition, trust, is the unspoken commodity of the canine-human relationship. In order to allow your dog to live in your home, you must be able to trust him not to eliminate inside, destroy your couch, or bite Aunt Sally. You trust that your dog's base animal instincts are quelled enough so that he seamlessly adapts to your world—life on the leash is a worthy trade-off for the comforts of home.

Of course, there's a flip side to my definition. Can your dog trust *you?*

Years ago I worked with a client, Bruce, who insisted that his Rhodesian Ridgeback, Sasha, jog with him every day, despite the fact that the dog was terrified of the cars passing by. Each time Sasha spotted a car on the horizon, she cowered and trembled and, as it came closer, the poor dog raced back and forth at the end of the leash, inconsolable. After cars passed, Sasha shook, panted, and refused to walk any farther, all the while scanning the horizon for more "monsters."

After seeing Sasha's dramatic fearfulness (it was the most extreme case I'd witnessed), I knew that I needed to have an uncomfortable conversation with Bruce. I couldn't understand why he continued running with Sasha when it was so clearly traumatizing her. Why would anyone voluntarily put a dog through that kind of stress on a daily basis? At first, I danced around my prognosis: "I understand how important your workouts are to you, but Sasha is really, really afraid out here. It's impossible to train her while she's so nervous, because her fear will prevent her from processing anything that we're trying to teach her. You just can't get through to a dog in this type of distress. In order to help Sasha get past this, we need to create a systematic training program. I'll map it all out for you, and we'll chip away at her fear together."

The look of concern on Bruce's face was not for the reason I expected. "How long is it going to take to fix this?"

"Well," I replied, "*fix* is a tricky word. These kinds of behavioral issues are like diabetes; you can treat them but you can't necessarily cure them. It's likely that she can overcome some of her fears, but I can't guarantee that it'll happen at the pace you're hoping for. Dealing with this level of fearfulness takes time, especially with such a pronounced reaction. Sasha has to set the pace, not you. That means that you'll have to hang up her running shoes for a while."

"Well, my wife and I do a five-mile run with her every weekend and we're not going to give that up. Sasha needs her exercise."

I was stunned. Was he not hearing me? Could he not see how stressed out his dog was? I decided to end the pleasantries and make my perspective perfectly clear.

"Sasha should not run though the neighborhood with you until there's a marked improvement in her reaction to cars. It's just not fair to her. If you can find a quiet park where you can run with her, do that instead. *I'll* help you understand when she's okay running on the street with you. Based on what I saw today, it won't be soon, and it definitely won't be by this Saturday."

I could tell by Bruce's demeanor that he wasn't buying my approach, and I prepared myself for the "thanks but no thanks" phone call that was to come after our lesson. I didn't have to wait long. Bruce told me that he was concerned that my slow and steady approach would be too drawn out, and that he really didn't want to stop running with his dog. He offered that if I could teach a technique that allowed him to continue running through his neighborhood with Sasha, then he'd be happy to work with me.

I couldn't do that.

Sasha required a methodical, dog-safe approach for dealing with her fear issues, but Bruce didn't have the patience to see it through. Granted, I've found that many people find it difficult to work through behavioral-modification programs, but what bothered me most was Bruce's lack of concern for Sasha's welfare. He knew that she was petrified during the daily runs, yet he didn't care. Could Sasha trust her owner to keep her out of harm's way? Absolutely not. Sadly, he put her there every day.

Regard

The final part of my definition of the bond, regard, is the most public face of the relationship between you and your dog. While the mutual respect and trust between you and your dog probably aren't on display at the dog park or during a leash walk, your dog's level of attentiveness toward you certainly is, and attentiveness is a sign of how your dog regards you. Are you all but invisible to your dog (like Daisy was with Beth), or are you the center of her universe (as Robert was to Cody)?

I'm not suggesting that you need that slavish sort of attention that you see at dog shows where the dog rarely looks away from the handler's face—it's unrealistic (and silly) to expect that laser focus in the everyday world. But it's critically important that your dog wants to check in with you and cares about your proximity to her no matter where you take her. Attentiveness is your dog's way of saying, "We're in this together, right?"

It's easy to train a dog to watch or look when you ask her to, but those learned behaviors aren't the same thing as straight-from-the-heart regard for you. A bonded dog looks to you because she *wants* to connect with you, not because you've asked her to. I once worked with a client who taught her young mixed-breed pup to glance up at her face when she said, "Watch." I was impressed the first time I saw it, but I soon realized that the word was a crutch for her. During walks, the pup was far more interested in the passersby on the sidewalk than he was in his person, so the woman compensated by saying, "Watch! Duke! Duke! Watch!" every four steps. Duke dutifully swung his eyes to meet hers each time she asked, collected his treat, then went right back to ignoring her. The cycle continued for the entire walk, until Duke tired of treats and decided to ignore his person's never-ending requests for attention. In this case, Duke had been taught to check in with his person, but he only did so begrudgingly, when she asked. I never saw Duke look up at his person to check in on his own. Unfortunately, he only did it when he was getting "paid," not because he wanted to.

I like the word *regard* because it encompasses a few elements of the bond: attentiveness, concern, and esteem. The word *regard* suggests a relationship based on mutual well-being, and an investment in one another. That is, in a nutshell, the very core of the bond.

What a Strong Bond Can Do

With my attempted deconstruction of the bond complete, let's dive into the fun stuff. Once you've grown a titanium bond with your dog, what's next? What does a strong bond do for you and your dog?

No bad dogs

When I go to social events and people find out that I'm a dog trainer, someone inevitably says, "Oh, I tried training my dog, but she's just so naughty! I swear, she knows how to do sit and down, but she only does them when *she* wants to!" Sounds like someone needs a bond intervention!

Once you've assessed your relationship and worked on your bond, you won't have to use the excuse, "She knows how to do it—she's just stubborn," to explain away your dog's misbehavior. I've heard some of my former clients use that line, and it chafes me because the seeming insubordination usually isn't just the dog's fault. For some reason, obedience training is often viewed purely as "tricks," or cute little behaviors that a dog will do in order to obtain a promised treat in a very controlled scenario (for example, doing a sit in the kitchen in order to get a cookie before bed every night). Your dog may seem to become "stubborn" when you ask to her to sit when her favorite neighbors want to greet her; instead, she responds by jumping.

But think about it: Have you ever practiced sit in that type of distracting environment? Has your dog even attempted a sit outside the four walls of your house? Does she know how to sit when faced with people who are excited to see her and eager to pet her? The bonded dog has a sit vocabulary that works at your friendly neighbor's house and beyond.

Sweet freedom

A strong bond is your dog's passport to the world. The "bad dog" has to stay home because she can't contain herself in the car, or she makes a spectacle of herself at the pet store; the bonded dog gets to accompany you anywhere you'd like to take her. While the bonded dog is out and about, she's attentive to you and well-mannered. She's a welcoming host to your guests. Instead of jumping up on them at the front door and harassing them as they sit on the couch, she greets them with good cheer and gentle affection, and then goes about her business. The bonded dog is the ultimate canine ambassador.

How touching

"Oh, I can't trim my dog's nails. She hates it when I touch her feet. And brushing her? Are you kidding?!"

Sound familiar? I get nervous when I hear about dogs who won't let their owners handle them. *Touch intolerance* (which is something entirely different from *touch avoidance,* due to undiagnosed pain) suggests a lack of trust. Physically connecting with your dog, whether for affection or basic care like nail clipping and tooth brushing, is a critical part of your relationship. After all, if you can't touch your own dog, how do you expect your vet or groomer to do it?

Touch for a treat

Is your dog funny about having certain parts of her body (like her feet or neck) handled? This strategy can help her get over some of her handling sensitivity by teaching her that she can earn treats for allowing you to gently touch her.

Start working on a neutral area on you dog's body that's far away from the "hot zone." If she's sensitive about her feet, start with her shoulders. Gently touch your dog's shoulder for a second, and then deliver a meaty treat with the opposite hand. Repeat the process several times, changing the duration of the touch and adding unpredictable pauses so that your dog doesn't pick up on a rhythm. Gradually work your way down your dog's leg, touching and then treating, until you can quickly touch her foot without provoking a reaction.

For a more detailed look at this body-handling process, check out *Mine!: A Practical Guide to Resource Guarding in Dogs,* by Jean Donaldson (Kinship Communications).

Note: Some handling issues have nothing to do with the strength of the bond with your dog. A rescued dog with a history of painful nail trims, or a dog who has undiagnosed back issues, will likely react poorly to handling.

My Sumner detests having his nails clipped (he howls like a baby before the clipper even touches a nail), but he begrudgingly allows me to do it without a fight. (His dramatic editorial comments as I clip make me giggle, and he seems to know that. He's a ham.) Sumner was recently bleeding from the mouth, and it was clear that he wasn't feeling well, but I was able to inspect the inside of his mouth thoroughly until I discovered the source of the injury.

Zeke's dysplastic back hips pain him when he runs too much, but I can relieve some of his pain with gentle massage, right near his most tender areas. I can tell my touch is uncomfortable for him at first by the way his eyes move and by his breathing patterns (more on reading your dog's body language in chapter 3), but he works through the pain, as if he knows the unpleasantness will decrease as his muscles relax.

My dogs allow me full body access because we have a strong bond based on trust, and they know that my touch brings good things.

You drive me crazy

You didn't bring a dog into your home thinking that your relationship would be a source of conflict and frustration, but somehow, here you are. You enrolled in a six-week training course back when your dog was a pup, you take her on a fifteen-minute walk twice a day, and you just can't understand why things aren't turning out as you'd planned. You're embarrassed by your dog's behavior. You're at the end of your rope. "I wanted Lassie," you think. "How did I end up with *this* dog?" Enter, the bond. It's time to turn your confrontational relationship into a symbiotic one.

I'm not saying that strengthening the bond with your dog will release you from any and all frustration you might feel when it comes to your canine best friend. I think that my dogs are pretty amazing, but they still do things that make me simmer. For example, they love to fence-fight with the dog who lives behind us. There's nothing I can do to override their drive to make the neighbor dog's life unpleasant when she's in her backyard. Though I can't stop the unmannerly behavior from kicking in, I can short-circuit it as soon as it begins. I've trained them to respond to a whistle, so as soon as I hear a hint that a backyard rumble is afoot, I give it a toot and watch them sail back to me. They've gotten better and better at returning to me when I whistle, so a once annoying behavior has become an exercise in advanced training. It's actually an impressive recall now! My minor frustrations with my dogs exist, but our strong bond makes them manageable.

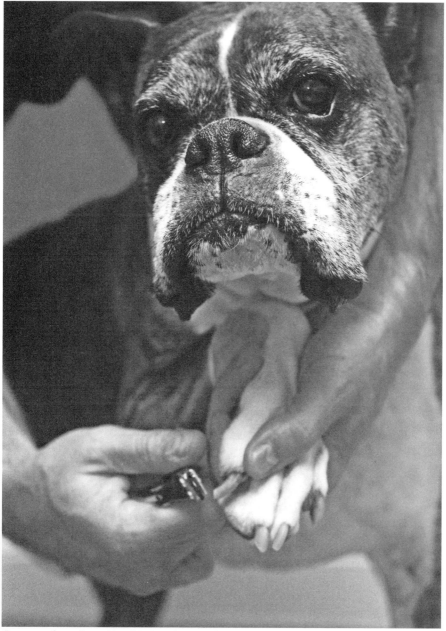

Sumner doesn't enjoy having his nails clipped, but he tolerates it without a struggle.

Is It Ever Too Late to Build a Bond?

Want the short answer?

No.

Of course, many factors can impact the speed of the bonding process, and the ultimate strength of your new bond. Your history with your dog will play a major part. If you've had an ongoing human-versus-dog attitude that led you to physically discipline your dog using intimidation and pain-based techniques (like spanking, alpha rolls, scruff shakes, choke chains, or electronic collars), I can guarantee that it'll take time to heal the damage done.

In a formerly punitive household, the dog needs to learn to trust her owner again. The beauty of making the switch from traditional training to a more positive approach is that, once you begin, everything snowballs in the best possible way. It's as if you've flipped a switch in your dog that suddenly enables her to act like a dog, not a robot. Your dog will have a new spring in her step and, once she's learned to trust again, a new regard for you. I've seen it happen with my own eyes, and it's a beautiful thing.

Your dog's age will impact the process as well. Nine years of ignoring you at the dog park when it's time to leave won't turn around magically overnight—that's a lot of history to undo! Now, I am in no way suggesting that older dogs are incapable of changing—you *can* teach an old dog new tricks. I am saying, though, that an older dog might be more set in her ways and used to life as she knows it. Growing the bond with an older dog takes patience.

Although it's difficult for me to admit it, your dog's breed will also play a part in the process. Why is it difficult to admit? Because I'm not "breedist." When I train, I always try to see the individual dog before me rather than a set of breed characteristics on four legs. I believe that too much canine misbehavior is written off due to breed types. When I hear,

Old-school training: Don't try this at home

An *alpha roll* is an outdated training technique used to discipline a dog that is perceived to be misbehaving. The dog is flipped onto her back and held there by her chest or neck until she calms down and "submits" to the owner.

A *scruff shake* is a behavioral correction that requires the owner to grab the sides of the dog's neck, glare into the dog's eyes, and shout "No!"

An *electronic collar*, also known as an *e-collar* or *tap collar*, is a training tool that delivers a painful shock through two contact points at the dog's throat when the owner perceives that the dog is acting inappropriately.

"My dog will never be able to walk politely on a leash—she's a Husky," I don't buy it. Sure, it might be more challenging to teach a Husky to walk close to you due to her genetic predisposition to pull, and you'll need to be more committed to the process, but it's certainly not *impossible* to teach a northern breed to walk with poise. (Give your dog some credit!) That said, I can't be blind to the fact that breed characteristics *do* play a part in the strength of the bond. Some breeds don't crave physical affection and closeness. Some are loners. Some are standoffish. Some are "programmed" to perform a job. Some might prefer to bond to just one person in the household, and maybe for now it's not you.

Not every dog breed falls under the goofy, let-me-smother-you-with-kisses umbrella of canine behavior. My bonding suggestions won't necessarily turn an aloof dog into a cuddler—you can't change your dog's temperament. In keeping with my "I'm not a breedist" stance, I still believe that even the less demonstrative breeds or the born-to-work breeds can grow an enviable bond with their person. It just might take longer, and it might not be as flashy.

Some dog-human matches never should have happened, and those odd couples might also find the bonding process more challenging. Years ago, I worked with a young woman who lived in a studio apartment in the city and who had a thriving social calendar that involved happy hours and late nights, and a—wait for it—six-month-old Border Collie. A don't-fence-me-in, on-the-job, born-to-problem-solve Border Collie. When I asked her why she opted to bring home a high-drive breed given her busy lifestyle and tiny apartment, she told me that she "liked how they look."

Reassessing the relationship

It's not easy to admit that you might have made a mistake when you selected your dog. If you've determined that your match isn't a healthy one—for you or your dog—there's no shame in considering rehoming her. If you can't give a dog the time or attention she deserves, rehoming is the most humane solution.

Be honest about the reasons why you're relinquishing your dog as you complete the paperwork so that the adoption coordinators can find an appropriate new home. Fibbing about your dog's behavioral traits (like covering up if she's not good with other dogs, or if she's not potty trained) is unfair to both the dog and future adopters. Consider breed-specific rescue if you have a purebred dog, or a nationwide organization like Petfinder (www.petfinder.com).

If you made an uninformed breed choice but you're 100 percent committed to keeping your dog no matter the circumstances (a potentially unwise decision in some scenarios), recognize that you're going to have to work harder and longer at growing your bond. It's difficult enough to do the right thing for your dog in the best circumstances (when you have ample free time, plenty of yard space, and robust health), but when you're saddled with a long workday that doesn't leave time for your dog, or you live in a dog-unfriendly environment, or you're not physically able to give your dog enough exercise, you have to put in extra effort to see that your dog somehow gets what she needs and then some.

Newer rescue dogs with baggage might seem bond-resistant at first. The shy dog, the skittish dog, and the dog with too many issues to name will be suspicious and untrusting for reasons that probably have nothing to do with you. Your bonding process will require a great deal of patience. I liken it to a dance, with your dog acting as Fred Astaire to your Ginger Rogers. Fred led the dance, Ginger followed, and the same goes for you and your dog. It's important that shy dogs be allowed to set the pace for training and behavioral-modification programs. Pushing shy dogs out of their comfort zone, or asking too much of them, can halt the process.

I once worked with a couple who had just adopted an extremely shy 4-year-old Dachshund, Millie. The husband respected the dog's timidity and let her approach life at her own pace, but the wife was eager to cement the relationship with her new best friend. She pushed poor Millie with a good-natured relentlessness. The wife reached for Millie when the dog retreated under the ottoman, and pulled the now stiff-as-a-board dog onto her lap for cuddle time. As the weeks passed, the wife couldn't understand why Millie sought out her husband over her. His trust-building patience was just what Millie needed.

All of the previous gloom and doom doesn't change the fact that if you want to strengthen your relationship with your dog, you can. It's never too late, your dog is never too old, and your scenario is never too screwed up to commit to nurturing a stronger relationship. The process will be subtle. You might experience gains that are two steps forward, one step back—which can be frustrating—but have confidence in the fact that you're making progress and your relationship is changing for the better.

Both you and your dog will feel the change, and be happier for it.

A strong bond is a good thing for you and your dog!

Chapter 2

WAYS WE ACCIDENTALLY UNDERMINE THE BOND

immediately noticed the choke chain around the neck of Buster the Portuguese Water Dog. It was hard to miss, given that his owner, Eric, kept yanking it and shouting "No! Stop it!" What was the infraction that warranted Eric's stern rebukes? Buster was a front-door fanatic: He became anxious and menacing every time someone rang the doorbell. These types of greetings were the very reason I was there. My introduction to Buster and Eric was intense, both because of Buster's scary reactivity toward me and because of Eric's anger as he tried to deal with it.

I tried to remember my initial phone conversation with Eric. Had I mentioned that I'm a positive trainer, and that I don't practice old-school training techniques? Eric didn't seem at all sheepish about delivering the corrections to his dog, so I assumed that my conversation with him had been rushed and I hadn't had a chance to explain my stance on choke collars. "This is going to be interesting," I thought.

Rather than jump right in and condemn the choke collar and traditional training I was witnessing, I began the session with my standard Q&A, all the while watching how Buster interacted with Eric and his

Not correct at all

A *correction* is part of a punishment-based traditional dog-training technique. The dog is fitted with a linked metal collar that is usually connected to a leash. When the dog doesn't respond as the handler wants, the leash is quickly pulled tight, thereby delivering a corrective jerk to the collar around the dog's neck. The dog learns that when he makes a misstep, he will be punished with a collar correction. Not every dog reacts to traditional training as negatively as Buster did. Many breeds with thick necks seem oblivious to the choking action.

wife, Linda. Buster struck me as a subdued dog, despite his blustery greeting at the front door. He almost seemed suppressed. He opted to sit close to Linda, who stroked him gently as we chatted. Buster ignored me, which was surprising—most dogs can't resist a friendly stranger who shows up at their house bearing treats, toys, and chews.

Eric was eager to show off the training he'd done with Buster. "Sit!" He commanded. "Now, down! Down!" Buster was slow to go into the down position, so Eric hooked his finger in the choke chain and yanked it toward the ground. I cringed, knowing that Buster's reluctance to perform the behavior was probably due to the fact that I was sitting close by, and that he didn't have a comfortable space in which to assume the position.

I gingerly asked Eric about the choke chain.

"We're a very traditional household," Eric replied. "We've trained all our dogs using these collars, and they've all been great animals. It works for us. It helps our dogs understand that we're the alphas in the household."

Alpha. I shuddered at the word. To me, *alpha* is the dirtiest concept in dog training. It reeks of everything I despise in old-school training. Be the alpha dog, the master. *Make* your dog obey. The problem I have with the alpha concept—aside from the punishing training techniques required—is that there's no sense of partnership between dog and human in the alpha school of thought. I reined in my initial visceral response and plodded on.

A choke chain is a painful, outdated training tool.

"Well, I have to be honest with you," I replied. "I don't use choke chains, and I don't like them. I'm sorry if I didn't make that clear during our phone call. The traditional training you've done with your dogs—the kind that uses choke collars—certainly has a strong history, but the method I use is a more modern, dog-friendly take on training. The goal is to make the training process straightforward and fun for Buster, and I hope for you as well! I have to be honest with you: What I'm seeing right now is a dog who looks pretty short on fun. . . ."

I knew I had an ally in Linda when she piped up and agreed with me. She didn't come out and say it, but I could tell that the old-school training method wasn't sitting well with her, despite her history with it. Eric, on the other hand, looked dubious.

"Are you willing to try it?" I asked. "I mean, I'm here, after all. Let's just give it a shot."

So we did, and I wasn't at all surprised to see Buster emerge from his shell. This dog, who just twenty minutes before had seemed shut down and broken, became outgoing and confident as the lesson progressed. Linda seemed thrilled by both the dog-friendly training approach and the results we were getting. *I* was thrilled to see Eric interacting differently with Buster as we moved through the lessons. His furrowed brow softened, and a playfulness replaced the "be the boss" attitude he'd had when I'd first arrived. The entire vibe of the household changed over the course of our lesson, and it manifested most obviously in the canine member of the family. Wagging, dancing, smiling—Buster was finally acting like a normal 2-year-old dog. Positive training saves the day!

We don't set out to damage our relationships with our dogs, but unfortunately, it's not hard to do. In Eric's case, outdated training advice and the idea that he needed to be the boss at all costs had adversely affected his bond with his dog. Though Buster was compliant and did what he was told the majority of the time, the heavy-handed nature of Eric's training had all but snuffed the spirit out of the dog. More telling was the fact that the corrections being delivered at the front door weren't having an impact on Buster's reactivity. The level of collar choke necessary to permanently override Buster's intense reactivity probably would have leveled the poor dog. Thankfully, few dog owners have the stomach to deliver that kind of blow. The result is the ineffective, persistent collar chokes that pick away at the bond between dog and person one yank at a time.

Correcting a reactive dog is essentially taking the ticker off the time bomb. Explosive reactions like Buster's are a warning, or a way for the dog to say, "I'm letting you know that something isn't right here." Punishing a highly aroused dog with collar chokes is telling him that his bluster is unacceptable, but it does nothing to change the emotion behind it. In the future, when pushed to the limit, the punished dog may bypass his very obvious barky warning—because he'll be punished for it—and go straight to a bite.

Much damage is done to the human-canine bond in the name of training. Outdated advice, myths, and ignorance all play a part. Your aging vet tells you that the best way to train a dog not to jump on people is to knee the dog in the chest, so you dutifully comply. You watch that TV dog trainer demonstrate a neck pinch on an aggressive dog, and you assume that it's a legitimate training technique. But take a moment and ask yourself, "Does this *feel* right for my dog?" No matter who is dispensing the advice, listen to your gut. If it feels wrong for you and your dog, it probably is.

When I began my dog training career, I apprenticed with a trainer who only used choke chains. I was cowed by his blustery, know-it-all attitude, so I went along with his methods. Or I tried to. I remember the first time I came home from working with him and tried to apply what I'd learned on my dog Zeke. I'll never forget Zeke's face the first time I delivered a correction. He looked at me with an expression that said, "*What* the. . . ? That was *so* uncool!" And it was. I felt terrible about delivering a blow for an infraction as mild as straying a bit too far while leash walking, and I never used the choke collar on him again. After watching me attempt to train client dogs using the choke-collar method, the old trainer decided that I was "too soft" to

Ask yourself, "Does this feel right for my dog?"

train adult dogs (because I didn't have the heart to deliver hard enough corrections) and suggested that I carve out my training niche working puppies.

There was a time when force-based dog training was the only option available, but the tide changed in the mid-1980s. Dog training pioneers, drafting off the stunning success of scientists like B. F. Skinner, Keller Breland, Marian Breland Bailey, and Bob Bailey, began incorporating scientific techniques like operant conditioning with great success. *Operant conditioning* is a method of learning in which behavior is shaped by reinforcement or punishment. If I want to "shape" a dog to sit near me instead of jumping on me, I'll reward him with a treat every time he sits (which reinforces the sit) and leave the room every time he jumps on me (which is a punishment). Karen Pryor, a scientist, writer, and animal trainer, was the first dog trainer to bridge the gap between the scientific world and the dog-training general public, and she essentially gave birth to my method of choice, clicker training.

The old trainer had mentioned clicker training to me in passing. He dismissed it as fad. I was intrigued by the concept, so I decided to read up on it and see if it could be a viable training technique to add to my small bag of training tricks. I remember sitting at the kitchen table reading a short book

The clicker is a great behavior-building tool. Unfortunately, it doesn't function like a remote control.

about the method while Zeke sat next to me dozing. "This sort of makes sense to me," I thought as I read. I'd only gotten through about fifteen pages before I decided to pick up the clicker and actually try it out with Zeke.

Zeke had a good understanding of the basic obedience concepts at that point, but tricks were lost on him. I'd spent months trying to teach him to roll over by physically manipulating his body through the process, but he'd always wind up stiff and unhappy. I simply couldn't figure out how to *make* my dog learn to roll over. I figured that the frustrating rollover process would be an excellent test bed for clicker training.

Click by click, I turned my roll-resistant dog into a trick fanatic. He figured out how to execute the roll within minutes! He loved the process, and we quickly added a high-five and wave to his repertoire. I was stunned by his joyful reaction to the training, which stood in stark contrast to my experience attempting to train him with the choke collar. It took a third of a book, twenty-five minutes, and a simple party trick to formally convert me to a full-time clicker trainer.

Though old-school training holdouts still exist, particularly in rural areas, clicker training hit the dog community in a big way, and millions of dogs are happier for it. In recent years, animal handlers and trainers at zoos and aquariums discovered clicker training and are successfully using operant-conditioning techniques on everything from water-dwelling devil rays to rhinos. Where the handlers once used force to manage the creatures in their facilities, they're now training the animals to take part in their own care. Before operant conditioning, the handlers used fire hoses or hooked sticks to move the animals from one area of their enclosure to another. Now, using clicker training, they teach them to move through their enclosures of their own volition, and reward them for their efforts.

Clicker training at a glance

Clicker training is based on operant conditioning. The clicker, a matchbook-size plastic toy, serves as a marker to clearly communicate to your dog when he has performed the action that will pay off with a food reward. The sound of the click is far more precise than verbal praise, so your dog has a clear understanding of exactly why he gets his reward. As your dog masters the commands, the precise click is no longer needed to communicate "That's it!" At that point, you can wean your dog off the clicker. (When I write the word *click,* it's synonymous with *click and treat.*)

I was fortunate enough to witness a behind-the-scenes training session at a zoo with a panda bear. The panda was trained to place his arm out through the bars of his enclosure into a hollow chute and hold it there while the trainer drew blood. He had the option to withdraw his arm at any time—there was nothing securing him in the chute—but he waited until the trainer gave the "all done" cue to remove it. Before operant conditioning, zoo handlers had to sedate the animals just to draw blood, which resulted in testing inaccuracies. Now, the animals are willing participants in their own care. The patient, trusting interaction between the trainer and the panda was testament to the transformative power of operant conditioning.

This book isn't a training methodology comparison, though. I'm sold on dog-friendly, science-based training, and if you're still reading, you are, too!

Love You till It Hurts

I still cringe at the memory. I was walking my dogs, Zeke and Sumner, through the neighborhood, and we came up to "that house"—the one where the young yellow Lab spends too much time alone behind a fence in the backyard. Most days, he barked a surprisingly cheerful "hello" at us as we passed, but on this day, I was surprised to see that he was in the front yard unleashed and lumbering toward us. I immediately looked for escape routes, because Sumner has issues with free-range dogs. Seconds later, the Lab's owner appeared from the shadows and called him to come back. That big yellow goofball shocked me by turning almost immediately and heading back to her. I was impressed by the dog's good manners, and I was about to shout, "Nice work!" to his owner, just before I saw her take off her flip-flop and smack the dog on the head when he reached her.

"Did I just see that?" I thought to myself.

I strained to hear what she was saying to her dog as I passed, and I made out, "Bad dog—I told you not to run away." I was incredulous. Her dog had just done an amazing, distraction-filled recall, and she rewarded him with a whack to the skull! In that very moment, I had witnessed the makings of a recall-resistant dog—a dog who, when called, would think better of running up to his owner because, based on experience, he knew that it would probably end badly for him. But can you blame him? The Lab made a decision to ignore the tempting diversion we presented and run joyfully back to his owner, but he was rewarded for his efforts with a punishing blow. There was no excuse for her behavior and no defensible training methodology that would support her actions. She hit him *with her shoe*. My heart broke for the poor dog.

I'll say it clearly and without embellishment: *Physical punishment has no place in your relationship with your dog.* I don't care what the TV dog trainer, or your vet, or your neighbor says. Putting your hands on your dog in anger will do nothing but fracture your relationship. Ever heard that you should swat a puppy with a newspaper every time he messes in the house? Or that you should rub his nose in his mess? Those techniques are great for teaching your pup to be afraid of you, newspapers, and the act of elimination, but they'll do nothing to teach him where he *should* be pottying.

Puppies aren't born knowing that pottying inside isn't allowed—and whacking a pup with a newspaper isn't going to teach him where he should go.

Fido, Have Your People Call My People

I once worked with a corporate climber who had a young Lab. Craig's successes were evident: nice car in the driveway, big house in a desirable zip code, and a snazzy business wardrobe. His dog, Baxter, was a typical young Lab, with an exuberance that knew no bounds. Craig had summoned me to help him "get a handle on Baxter," a request I hear frequently. While I was quizzing Craig about his life with Baxter, the poor dog essentially vibrated before me with pent-up energy. Jumping, panting, pacing, pawing, and licking me for attention . . . poor Baxter couldn't seem to settle down enough to work on the bone I'd brought for him. He seemed ecstatic when he received any sort of attention from me, and he pretended as if Craig wasn't in the room. As my Q&A with Craig progressed, I began to understand why.

Craig's entire schedule revolved around work and the gym. He spent long days in the office, and frequently had business dinners with clients. When he wasn't on the clock, he was squeezing in a workout. In fact, it seemed like he was rarely home.

"What do you do about Baxter while you're gone?" I asked.

"Oh, I have a walking service. They come in once a day and give him a twenty-minute walk. Plus, I have a dog door, so Baxter can go outside whenever he wants. If I have to work really late, the service comes twice."

"Okay, so he gets a total of twenty to forty minutes of walking during the day. What about after you come home?"

"I'm usually dead tired at the end of the day, so I throw the ball for Baxter in the backyard for a little bit, we watch some TV, and then we just go to sleep. Well, *I* go to sleep—Baxter can't seem to settle down and he keeps me awake most nights," he laughed. "That's why you're here!"

"What about the weekends? You said that fitness is a big part of your life, so do you take Baxter for hikes in the park or something?"

"Well, I *would,* but he's so crazy on the leash that I can't control him! It's embarrassing! I go for hikes and bike rides most weekends, and Baxter hangs out here in the yard. That's when he digs those big holes, which are *another* reason why you're here!"

I had to bite my tongue to keep from asking Craig why he'd gotten a dog in the first place.

When you bring a dog into your life, you've essentially signed a contract stating that you have the time necessary to keep your dog happy and healthy, and that agreement extends far beyond a quick walk around the block once a day. Unfortunately, the parenting adage, "It's not the quantity, it's the quality," doesn't apply to dogs. Quantity counts, big time. One glorious fifteen-minute walk on a picturesque beach won't cut it unless you have a senior dog whose exercise needs have waned. Shipping your dog off to a training academy, not participating in his training, and then expecting perfection when your dog comes home is unrealistic. Making your dog live in the basement or, worse yet, out in the yard because you don't have the patience to potty-train him is unconscionable. Denying your dog the time he requires is unhealthy not only for him but for your relationship.

Work It Out

I ask every new client if they think their dog's exercise needs are being met, and nine out of ten people answer the same way: "Probably not"—without even thinking twice.

Craig's dog, Baxter, was an extreme example, but it's clear to me that even dogs in well-adjusted homes are suffering from an acute lack of exercise. For some reason, people operate under the assumption that dogs need only a short walk and a quick game of fetch to burn through their energy reserves. Not quite.

Drop it!

Many of my clients would love to play fetch with their dogs, but they're unable to because their dogs refuse to relinquish the ball. My client Ken mentioned in passing, when we were addressing his goals for training, that he wanted to teach his dog Bailey to play fetch, as if the concept was more of a fantasy than a teachable reality.

"Why is that?" I asked him. "Does she not like to play the game?"

"No, she loves playing with balls! She's a ball-crazy Jack Russell Terrier, but the problem is she won't give me the ball after she's gets it. Our games of fetch usually last one or two throws before she starts hoarding the balls and refusing to give them back to me. I know she wants to play fetch, but she just can't figure out how the game works."

"Ah, she needs to learn the Zen of fetch: To get the ball, you must give up the ball."

I gave Ken a quick fetch primer, and Bailey was soon fetching and releasing like a pro. Ken finally had a great way of exercising Bailey, and Bailey had a solid drop to add to her arsenal of skills.

Here's how you can do the same:

1. Put your dog on a leash and give him a ball. The leash will enable you to keep your dog from running off with the ball.

2. Take a high-value treat like cheese or meat and place it right in front of your dog's nose.

There's no standard for how much exercise a dog requires, but I can almost guarantee that your dog needs more than he's getting. Limiting your dog's daily exercise to taking short walks and playing the same predictable game is limiting the amount of fun you can have with your dog, and why would you want to do that? Having a good time with your dog is one of the easiest routes to building a strong bond. Again, exercise is a quantity *and* quality issue. Are you bored with the same old walk route and tired game of fetch in the backyard? Your dog probably is, too.

There's the oft-neglected part of the exercise equation: mental fatigue. Your dog needs to exercise his body, but that brain of his requires a workout as well. The good news about this forgotten exercise requirement is that you don't need a lot of space to perform it, and it doesn't take as long to meet your dog's requirement for it. If you play the *right* types of brain games (more on that later), you can mentally tax most dogs within a half-hour or less. I play a few different brain games with my dogs, and after fifteen minutes they're ready to take a break!

3. Most dogs will drop the ball in order to collect the treat, so say "drop" just as he releases the ball.

4. Pick up the ball and give it back to him, and then repeat the treat-in-front-of-nose process.

Make sure to have at least two similar balls when you're ready to try drop as a part of fetch. Throw the ball and encourage your dog to come back to you by squatting and clapping your hands. (I say, "Bring it!" as my dogs come running back to me.) He might hesitate when he's a few steps away from you—old habits die hard. Show him that you have another ball, which should encourage him to come closer to you. When he's right in front of you, say "drop" and offer either a treat or, if he's really ball driven, the other ball. If you've been practicing the drop, your dog should release the ball in his mouth, at which time you can throw the other ball. Lather, rinse, repeat, and you've got yourself a reformed ball hoarder!

Practice teaching the word *drop* in other scenarios as well—for example, if Fido picks up something unpleasant from the street or he finds your underwear in the laundry.

A tired dog is a good dog!

The unfortunate cycle that results from a lack of exercise is an under-stimulated dog looking to burn some energy who ends up creating mischief (barking, digging, destroying the house), and the angry owner who can't understand why her dog is acting out. If your dog is taxed, both mentally and physically, he won't need to find unsanctioned outlets for his energy because he won't have much energy left! It's a cliché because it's true: A tired dog is a good dog.

The Schoolyard Bully

I think we're all guilty of this infraction to some extent. Dogs' childlike, trusting manner makes them ripe for teasing.

"Want to go for a ride in the car, Fido? Huh? Do ya?"

Fido thinks, "Heck yeah!" and begins his happy dance.

"Too bad—just kidding!"

Teasing your pooch might get an easy laugh, but every time you do it, you're the person who cried wolf. Though not nearly as damaging as some of the other bonding infractions, this minor negative behavior chips away at your dog's trust in you over time. Plus, it's just not nice.

"Wanna go for a walk? Do you wanna?"

My guess is yes, your dog does want to go for a walk, so don't ask him unless you intend to make good on the offer.

Though teasing isn't a major bonding infraction, it does chip away at your bond over time.

Sir! Yes, Sir!

Gentlemen, I'm about to make a sweeping generalization, so please don't be upset with me for what I'm about to say. Some of you tend to act rather intense when it comes to interacting with your dog, particularly when it's training time. The words *drill sergeant* come to mind. Your foreheads furrow, your tone of voice takes on an edge, and the fun seems to drain from your body. I've seen it happen with women as well, so I won't heap *all* the blame on the men. Interacting with a dog who doesn't always listen seems to require an increase in decibels and a grumpy attitude. Instead of asking your dog to sit, you yell, "Sit! *Sit!*" Instead of calling your dog to come, you shout, "Fido, come!" with a growl in your voice. Why is that? Is your dog hearing impaired?

My former client Jack was guilty of this bonding infraction. I'd demonstrate an exercise with his dog, Milo, and then hand the dog off to him so that he could try it. Suddenly, Jack would morph from a smiling, fun-loving person into Captain Tough Guy. His military background shone through every time he told Milo to do something.

"Jack," I'd say with a grin, "is Milo a new recruit or something? You sound so angry!" I found a million different ways to cajole a smiling tone out of him during our lessons, and I had to hope that he didn't forget to keep it when he worked with Milo on his own.

Leash walks are particularly prone to Captain Tough Guy Syndrome. Making dogs *heel* (perform an ultraprecise leash walk in which the dog's head or shoulders are parallel to the handler's leg at all times, and forging ahead, lagging behind, or stopping to sniff are not allowed) somehow jumped from the competition obedience world and into the real world, to the chagrin of dogs everywhere who just want to stop and have a sniff now and then.

Heeling is unnatural outside of the show ring, and there's no reason to require it (there are no AKC judges hiding in your shrubbery), yet many of us persist, holding the leash tightly on the left and yanking our dogs back into place every time they take three steps too many. I always scrutinize dogs who are in lockstep with their people. Does the dog look like he's enjoying the walk? The glazed expression and disconnect from his surrounding points to "no."

Acting like a drillmaster rather than a partner will do nothing to strengthen the bond between you and your dog. You don't have to be a bossy, all-business alpha to grow the balanced relationship you're craving. Think back to your favorite teacher in school. Did you prefer the grumbling, quick-to-yell disciplinarian, or the caring, nurturing but strict teacher? Whom did you want to work harder for? Whom did you want to please?

Will You? Maybe? Please?

This next bonding infraction is going to sound like a contradiction to the last one. You need to maintain a positive, upbeat, nonmilitaristic manner when you're connecting with your dog, but you *also* need to project a certain amount of confidence in your tone and carriage. This is one of the more difficult bonding infractions to define, because it's less specific than any of the others. As they say about pornography and art, "I know it when I see it."

I definitely "knew it" when I worked with Catherine and her mixed-breed dog, Dolly. Catherine was a sweet person who clearly loved her dog very much. The problem was, when she interacted with Dolly, she was hesitant, as if she doubted her own abilities when it came to training her dog (who clearly adored her, but didn't really respect her). Instead of telling Dolly to sit, she'd say, "Now, Dolly, it's time to listen to me. Okay, Dolly? Ready? Ok, Dolly, siiiiittt. Dolly, siiit." Her posture looked positively concave. Meanwhile, high-energy Dolly was Hoovering her way around the room looking for dropped treats, ignoring Catherine's polite entreaties. The one time Catherine actually got Dolly to sit, she handed the treat over so slowly and with such timidity that Dolly looked as if she wasn't sure if she was even *getting* a treat.

My advice to Catherine: "Try standing straighter, and instead of begging Dolly to sit, ask her to do it as if you really mean it. She knows what the word means now, so when you're ready for her to sit, just get her attention and say the word, like this. . . ." I whistled once, which snapped Dolly out of her treasure hunt. The moment she looked at me I said, "Good girl!" She walked over to me, and when she was close and her focus was on me I said, "Sit." One word, one time, and she did it like a champ.

"You have to be confident that she knows what the word means, and that she wants to work for you. She *does* want to work for you, Catherine, there's just too much static around you right now. Mean what you say, and say what you mean. Try it."

Catherine took my advice to heart and attempted another sit with Dolly. This time she straightened her back and said "sit" with a quavering authority in her voice. I could tell that she still didn't believe in herself, but Dolly managed to nail the sit. Catherine glowed.

The rest of our lessons were a strange dance of me trying to lead by example and Catherine doing her best to leap out of her comfort zone. She was soft-spoken and passive by nature. It was clear that requiring her to speak with confidence was awkward for her.

Dolly's affection for Catherine was tempered by the fact that she knew she could push Catherine around. When Dolly wanted to sniff something far off the path, she merely bulldozed through and dragged a stuttering Catherine behind her. When Dolly felt like she wasn't being rewarded frequently enough during a walk, she bumped her nose against Catherine's leg until Catherine relented and gave her a treat.

I tried to point out instances where Catherine was being a pushover, but I began to feel guilty about my goading to get her to become something she wasn't. She committed so many little infractions that to point them all out would seem petty. However, their combination created a "power vacuum" that Dolly eagerly occupied.

I've dealt with many wishy-washy clients, and it's always difficult for me to try to tell them that part of the reason their dog isn't that into them is because they aren't that into themselves. Dogs are more perceptive than we give them credit for. They can spot a pushover and very quickly figure out how to work the situation to their advantage. (Despite what the Lassie myth sold us about dogs wanting to please us, the truth is that dogs are self-motivated opportunists.) Self-assuredness is legal tender in the dog world.

Again, suggesting that you act confident with your dog isn't granting you license to go the alpha route. There's a difference between acting like a drill sergeant and acting like a gentle leader. The dogs I work with understand that I'll give them clear direction, that I mean what I say, and that they'll be richly rewarded for working with me. They appreciate the clarity.

On Second Thought . . .

It's Sunday and you're camped out on the couch reading the paper. Your dog gives you that pleading look that seems to say, "The floor could not be *any* harder this morning, and your lap looks so very lovely," and you relent. After all, it's Sunday—to heck with the rules! You can go back to the no-couch stuff on Monday. And while you're at it, you may as well let your dog have a bite of your bagel. . . .

Then Monday rolls around too soon and you're nearly out the front door when you notice your dog stretched from end to end on the couch. He's grinning at you. "Life is grand, ain't it?"

Though dogs are excellent timekeepers, they don't understand that certain days of the week allow for a relaxation of the rules. An invitation to come up on the couch on Sunday is as good as a free pass for the rest of the week. It's not fair to subject your dog to your changing whims and then expect him to understand why something that was okay the day before no longer is. It's important not only to make household rules, but to stick with them. Dogs thrive on consistency and predictability.

Another common blurring of the rules occurs with jumping up. You invite Fido to jump up and give you a hug when you're wearing your after-hours gear, but you forbid it when you're dressed for work. Unless you teach Fido a specific cue that gives him the okay to jump on you, he'll never be able to understand why you welcome some hugs but refuse others.

It's fine to let your dog join you on the couch, but if you decide to disallow it, be consistent about that rule.

Pre-K to Grad School in Just One Week!

"Victoria, we practiced recalls around the house with our dog a few times after our first lesson. Then we took him to the dog park and tried it but he wouldn't listen!"

I hear that complaint frequently, which makes me pull out my big book of dog-training analogies to assist in my explanation: "Dog training is sort of like learning to read. You start off with the ABCs, then you move on to Dick and Jane, then you start reading books by Judy Blume, then you *eventually* get to Tolstoy. When you took your dog to the dog park after only doing a few days of basic recalls, you essentially jumped from the ABCs straight to Tolstoy."

To be successful, training should be an incremental process. Dogs are great at learning new behaviors, but they need coaching to learn to generalize those behaviors to new environments. A sit in the kitchen is something entirely different from a sit at the vet's office. The problem arises when people assume that, because their dogs know how to sit at home, they should be able to do it everywhere, in every scenario. If the dog can't do it successfully, it must be because he's being stubborn.

The same goes for that dog-park recall. Your dog may be the master of the backyard recall, but there's not as much competing interest in your backyard as there is at the dog park. New bottoms to sniff, new people to greet, new squirrels to chase—the dog park is a different *planet!* The key to training success is to try to view the world from a dog's perspective and take distractions into account. *You* might think that the sidewalk outside the coffee shop is the exact same as the sidewalk outside your front door, but your dog begs to differ.

How about an example? Say you become an excellent ice-skater by practicing all alone on a small pond in the country. You teach yourself a mean triple Axel, and you can Salchow with the best of them. Your audience consists only of cardinals and chickadees. One day, a talent scout discovers you and offers you the chance of a lifetime: a slot on the Olympic figure-skating team. Your first competition is tomorrow. You sign on—you're an *excellent* skater after all. Before you know it, your performance is about to begin, and you're understandably nervous. You remind yourself that you're an *excellent* skater. You skate to the center of the distractingly smooth ice and wonder why all those helpful bumps that dimpled the surface of your practice pond are missing. There's a deafening roar surrounding you, a thousand voices, 2,000 eyes. Flash photography everywhere. You feel dwarfed by the size of the arena—you could skate from one end of your practice pond to the other in just twenty paces. HD cameras capture the sweat stains forming under your arms. Suddenly you're jolted by music that you can feel in your chest. It distracts you, and you stand on the ice motionless for a full ten seconds as you try to figure out how to match the music you're hearing on the loudspeakers to the music you've been playing in your head for the past ten years.

Suddenly, you're not such an excellent skater.

That's sort of what happens with our dogs when we expect them to seamlessly transition from a known environment to an unfamiliar one. The skill sets are still there—your dog hasn't "forgotten" how to sit, just as the skater still knows how to Salchow—it's just that he hasn't learned how to perform in that new arena yet. Every time you're tempted to write off your dog's refusal to sit at the vet's office as disobedience, remember the fish-out-of-water ice-skater and commit to helping your dog learn to perform in the new venue.

White-Glove Service

Many of my clients admit to spoiling their dogs, but when I ask them for specifics, they usually list benign behaviors like letting the dog sleep in their bed, cuddling too much, or letting him lick the plates after dinner. Zeke and Sumner's dirty paws and snoring habits keep me from inviting them into bed, but as for allowing them to clean plates before we load the dishwasher and giving them drawn-out massages? Guilty as charged.

Sleeps with dogs

Many of my clients guiltily admit that they allow their dogs to sleep in bed with them, and then wait for me to scold them for it. I don't. There's a persistent dog-training myth that suggests that allowing your dog to join you on the couch or in bed causes your dog to become ascendant and claim ownership of your entire domain. That's simply untrue.

When I suggest that spoiling your dog will negatively impact the strength of your bond, I'm talking about insidious little undesirable behaviors that add up and shift the balance of your relationship with your dog. The "mutual respect" portion of my bond definition is missing in these types of relationships—truly spoiling your dog is sort of like giving him permission to be a furry dictator.

It's not always evident to the human side of the relationship, as my canine client Misha proved to me. Within the first two minutes of our meeting, I figured out that he loved to play ball. It was impossible to avoid the dirty, slobber-soaked ball that he kept dropping in my lap as I chatted with his person.

"*So* sorry," Wanda said to me, as I removed the ball from my lap and set it on the ground for a third time. "Misha, bring it here."

Wanda then threw the ball across the room for Misha and continued to do so for the entire twenty minutes we sat and talked. If the ball rolled under the couch, Misha stood in front of it and barked at Wanda until she retrieved it for him. If Wanda took too long to throw the ball, Misha barked at her and then pawed her arm. The flow of our conversation was constantly interrupted by Misha's ball-throwing requirements, but Wanda seemed oblivious to it.

Misha had trained his person well.

The spoiled dog is the bossy dog, as was the case with Misha. Have you caught yourself saying, "He barks at me when he's hungry," or, "We get up when he gets up." In those scenarios, *he's* setting the household rules and making *you* adhere to them. So much for mutual respect! A healthy dog-human relationship has a "you scratch my back and I'll scratch yours" element to it. You do things for your dog (provide food, shelter, playtime, and so on), and he returns the favor by doing things for you (sitting when you ask him to and refraining from eating the couch, for example). The spoiled dog only believes in half of that equation—and I bet you can guess which half.

Spoiling seems to be particularly common in petite breeds. There's the Yorkie who gets carried everywhere, the Chihuahua who doesn't know how to sit when asked because "he's so small that he doesn't have to know how to do it," and the Toy Poodle who can make a grown man move from his favorite spot on the couch with just a hard stare. Size isn't an excuse for overindulging a dog.

Spoiling creeps into relationships initially under the guise of affection. It's normal to want to make life comfortable and easy for your dog. Feel free to love your dog to pieces—just make sure that it's not a case of your dog getting something for nothing.

May I Speak to a Manager, Please?

Dave and Maureen were having an impossible time potty-training their new puppy Jasper. Seems the little guy let fly in the kitchen whenever the mood hit, and, to top it off, Jasper was now adding furniture chewing to his list of tricks. When they called me, they said they thought that Jasper was exceptionally difficult to housetrain, and they were considering banishing him to the backyard until he "figured out where to potty."

They led me into the kitchen to meet Jasper, and I understood the problem immediately. Jasper, an 11-week-old puppy, had free reign of the entire room and all the tempting goodies within. There was no puppy-proofing to speak of. Jackets and shoes were tossed on the floor near the door, chairs were piled high with newspapers, and the garbage can was peeking out from beneath the sink. I was amazed that Jasper hadn't done *more* damage given his surroundings!

Contain yourself

You feel guilty about putting your dog in a crate, so you assuage that guilt by buying the biggest one you can find. Unfortunately, that strategy is going to backfire. The crate should be sized so that your dog can comfortably stand up, turn around, and lie down in it, but it shouldn't be any bigger. The more floor space in your dog's "condo," the more area he has to make a deposit in one corner and sleep dry and comfortable in the other.

I was happy to see that Dave and Maureen had an appropriately sized crate in the kitchen, and I asked them about it. "I hate putting him in the crate. I feel guilty! Isn't it cruel to lock him in there?" Maureen asked me.

"It's crueler to leave him out, running free," I replied. "He won't learn how to hold it and wait to potty outside, which means he'll continue to have accidents, which will continue to make you angry and frustrated, and the cycle will go on until you decide that a 6-month-old dog who's still pooping in the house isn't worth the trouble. Keeping him outside in the yard won't help him figure out that he's not supposed to potty inside. He'll just continue to go when he feels the urge. Granted, he'll be in the correct location, but you won't be there to acknowledge him when he does it. And, to top it off, he'll probably start landscaping your yard with holes because he's bored and lonely."

A little bit of management in Jasper's world—a crate, better puppy-proofing, baby gates, and more supervision—would have easily turned a make-or-break housetraining crisis into a livable solution for all parties. Dogs—puppies in particular—don't intrinsically know how to fit into our world. Unless you teach Fido otherwise and set him up to succeed by managing his environment, your rug makes a fine toilet and that patent-leather pump you just kicked off is an excellent chew toy. It's up to us to teach them where to potty, what to chew, and how to interact with people. (That goes for adult dogs, too. It's a common misconception that an adult rescue dog knows where to potty because he's "old enough." If no one took the time to teach him, even though he's physically capable of holding it, he's as good as an 8-week-old puppy.)

Managing your dog's world is setting him up to succeed rather than allowing him to make mistakes and then punishing him for them. If your dog isn't able to resist the sandwich sitting on a low table, don't leave it there for him to steal. If your dog urinates on your Persian rug in the dining room every time he sneaks in there, cut off his access to the room by shutting the door, and go back to puppy-level housetraining using baby gates and more supervision. I often think of Albert Einstein's definition of insanity (doing the same thing over and over again and expecting different results) when my clients say things like, "Our dog tips over the garbage can *every day*." Those clients *know* that it's going to happen, but they do nothing to stop it from happening. Whose fault is that? Unfortunately, your dog doesn't have ESP, and he can't know what's expected of him by reading your mind. Proper household management and training are the only fair options.

Baby gates are a great way to help manage your dog's world.

Chapter 3

BONDING AND BODY LANGUAGE

Your dog would like to have a word with you.

Our dogs are *excellent* communicators, but their message gets lost in translation. That tail wag? It might not be the friendly invitation you think it is. The nonstop "kisses" your dog plants on your face? Adoration might not be the driving emotion behind it. The sad fact is that not enough of us take the time to learn to speak dog, and our relationships falter because of it. Your dog might look like she's playing with the vacuum when you pull it out when in fact she's actually petrified of it. Dogs talk—we don't always listen.

Touch-Aversive Dogs: Hands Off, Please!

One of the most common misinterpretations of dogspeak I've seen involves a basic dog/human interaction: petting. Think every dog enjoys it? Zeke begs to differ. Try to touch him, and he'll back away as if you're Animal Control on a neighborhood sweep. If Zeke had come from a rescue organization, well-meaning friends would probably suggest that his "hand shyness" was due to prior abuse. Having raised him since puppyhood, I know Zeke wasn't abused. He just doesn't want physical affection. Play? Bring it on. Touch? Keep your hands to yourself, please. For the first five years of his life, the only physical contact Zeke wanted with us were accidental cheek grazes on our hands during games of tug. It frustrated me—who doesn't want to pet and snuggle with their dog?—but I knew that forcing my affections on him wouldn't solve the problem. During Zeke's "hands-off" years, Sumner fulfilled my petting quota.

Zeke's not the only "differently wired" dog out there. Dogs who hang out in retail stores are forced to endure all sorts of touching, and many act as if they could do without being awakened from a nap by overzealous thumping.

Zeke avoided petting for the first five years of his life, but now he welcomes it.

The next time you run into a shop dog, take a close look at her while you pet her. Is she genuinely welcoming your touch, or just tolerating it? Stand back and watch how many people are oblivious to the dog's "look but don't touch" preference and follow behind her when she walks away. I've met many, many canine clients who prefer not to be petted, and, more often than not, their owners had no clue about that preference. I usually notice the dog's touch aversion at the first session when I gently reach out to her, only to have her back away. There are a number of reasons why a dog might move away from me at that first lesson, from shyness to overstimulation, so I usually ask the owner if his dog likes to be touched.

Nearly every owner says, "Of course!" And then they give me a funny look.

From that point on, I watch the interactions between dog and owner carefully, all the while trying my best not to make contact with the dog. It's not easy! (I think we're programmed to connect with fuzziness.) I watch to see if the dog solicits touch from anyone in the room. If I forget myself and accidentally pat the dog (hey, it happens), does she back away from me again or come closer and ask for more by putting her body or head next to my hand?

My recall exercise during that first lesson usually clues me in to the way the owner touches the dog, and what the dog thinks of that touch. I tell my clients to make a big deal when their dogs run up to them. "Have a party," I say. "You want your dog to think that she's a genius for what she just did!" My clients happily comply when their dogs get to them, giving hearty praise and, more often than not, big thumping pats on the head and back.

Often, my canine students' body language says, "Oh, no thanks! I'd prefer it if you *didn't* whack my head!" during the hearty petting, yet the owners persist, even reaching out for the dogs as they back away from their touch. A dog who doesn't appreciate that type of enthusiastic petting shows it in a number of ways, like moving away, ducking her head, dancing just out of reach, or even nipping and biting at the offending hands. Just imagine what this type of miscommunication does to your bond. Your dog is desperately trying to tell you that she doesn't appreciate your physical affection, and you're acting as if you're ignoring her pleas!

It's embarrassing to point out that a dog isn't enjoying her owner's petting. (People get a look on their faces that seems to say, "*How* did I miss that?") Instead of telling an owner to abandon the petting completely during the recall exercise, I suggest he try touching his dog on the chest or shoulders instead of the head, using a massaging touch instead of a thumping one. Some dogs appreciate the change in approach; others prefer to avoid touch completely during recall practice. (Coming when called can be a stimulating exercise, and many dogs would rather get paid with a treat and verbal praise than with touch.)

To make sure that the dog's petting aversion isn't due to training overstimulation, I tell my clients to track their dogs' desire for petting and physical contact during the week between the first and second lessons. Does the dog consistently back away or otherwise avoid petting? Does she enjoy gentle massage instead of traditional, walloping pats? Will she solicit more petting with her paws, head, or body when the petting stops? Many people are surprised to discover that the assumed foundation of the canine-human relationship, touch, isn't a given in *every* relationship.

The good news is that dogs can learn to enjoy petting if you take it slowly and really listen to what your dog is telling you with her body. In Zeke's case, I consciously abandoned all casual touching. (I did not, however, stop praising him and playing with him.) I made sure that he saw me giving Sumner physical affection, but I refrained from trying to touch him as well. It took months of this seemingly heartless behavior before I noticed Zeke edging closer to me when I gave Sumner massages. I'd reach out to Zeke, and if he didn't step back, I'd gently give him a few seconds of massage, all the while watching to see if he looked like he wanted to move away. I focused on his shoulders, a hard-working area that carries the bulk of his body weight due to his dysplastic back hips. Sometimes he'd move away after just a second or two, but occasionally he'd go into the down position to get more comfortable. Success! I always left him wanting more and stopped before he asked me to. Early on, I wasn't convinced that he was truly enjoying the touch—maybe it was just a ploy to get me to stop paying so much attention to Sumner!

Calming signals

Norwegian dog trainer Turid Rugaas identified yawning as a canine "calming signal," or a way that dogs communicate stress and attempt to defuse escalating situations. When you start actively looking for yawning dogs, you'll see them everywhere. My canine clients will yawn when their owners struggle to clip on the leash before a walk, or when we're outside walking and other dogs barge up to their faces to greet them.

This is an example of a stress yawn. Zeke was tired of being a model.

I watched his body carefully as I touched him. Leaning toward my touch, closing his eyes, and lapsing into to an awake-but-snoring slower breathing pattern were all excellent signs. Moving away was a no-brainer signal that he wasn't interested, as were more subtle hints, like keeping his body tense, flinching at my touch, yawning, and keeping his eyes wide open during the petting.

Zeke gradually accepted and began to enjoy shoulder massage, so I moved on to more creative locations. One of my most favorite spots to be massaged is on the top-middle part of my forearm up toward my elbow (try it—it feels amazing!), so I tried it on Zeke. It must feel good for dogs, too, because he quickly welcomed touch in that spot. Once I had made peace with his neck, shoulders, and front legs over the course of several months, I moved on to his belly and then, finally, much later, to those very tender, damaged back legs.

I knew that Zeke had learned to enjoy my touch the day he interrupted me as I petted Sumner. He walked over to us and very deliberately placed his paw on my hand as if to say, "My turn, please." I was elated. I welcomed this somewhat pushy request for physical affection because it was such a departure from his normal "Don't touch me" ways. He asked me to touch him! Manners be damned, I gave him what he wanted. A few weeks later he did the same thing to my husband, who *hadn't* been practicing gentle massage on him, and my eyes filled with tears. My strange, little, touch-aversive dog was generalizing his desire to be petted! Though he still backs away when he's overstimulated or faced with strangers who don't know about his petting quirks (he reverts back to play mode in those scenarios), he regularly asks both me and my husband for petting by either daintily reaching his paw out or rolling on his back and exposing his fat, pink belly. It's a beautiful thing.

Body Language Basics

There are many phenomenal books filled with the secrets of decoding canine body language. This book isn't one of them. I'm more interested in jump-starting your desire to observe your dog and attempt to take in what she's saying to you, but I'm just going to scratch the surface. You know your dog better than anyone, and if you pay attention (the missing link of communication), you can probably understand her more clearly than you realize.

The miscommunication that occurs without an understanding of dog-speak can undermine the strength of your bond over time. Just imagine how Zeke would feel about me if I continued to try to pet him despite his requests for me to stop. Your dog has learned to speak English (she knows what *sit, treat,* and *walk* mean, right?), so why not learn to speak a little dog and make life easier for both of you? Let's do some canine dissection.

The body as a whole

Tony called me a few months after we finished our basic training program with Zack because he was out of control every time they took him to the shopping plaza down the road from their house. I applauded their efforts to make Zack a part of the family and socialize him as much as possible. I assumed that Zack, an 8-month-old Lab mix, just needed help transitioning his basic training skills into real-world scenarios. We had worked primarily in the house, in the yard, and around the neighborhood during our initial training program, so I wasn't surprised that Zack was having difficulties applying his lessons in more distracting environments.

Learning to speak dog

Want to learn more about canine body language? Check out *On Talking Terms with Dogs: Calming Signals,* by Turid Rugaas (Dogwise Publishing), and *Off-Leash Dog Play: A Complete Guide to Safety & Fun,* by Robin Bennett and Susan Briggs (C&R Publishing).

The short walk to the plaza was pleasantly uneventful. It was clear that Tony had continued working with Zack after our lessons ended, because Zack was an excellent leash walker. He opted to keep his pace close to ours, and, though he raced ahead when a squirrel dared to cross his path, he fell back in step with us a few seconds later. I was impressed. Unfortunately, everything changed as we got closer to the shops.

Zack's carriage seemed to collapse. His loose, waggy body posture disappeared and was replaced by low, slow, slinking movements. Instead of walking next to us on the sidewalk, he moved as close as he could to the brick wall near the edge of the parking lot. Once we entered the shopping area, he began racing back and forth at the end of the leash with his rear end tucked in so tightly that his bottom nearly dragged on the ground. Tony had a hard time holding onto the leash, and he nearly knocked over several pedestrians as he tried to control Zack. This fabulous dog who was so in tune with us on the way to the plaza was now completely disconnected.

"See what I mean?" Tony asked. "He's a total nut-job! He gets so excited when we come here that I can't get through to him. It's like we never trained him at all!"

What I saw in Zack wasn't a training disconnect, but a dog in deep distress. Zack's body language—his low carriage, the pace that alternated between tortoise-slow and frantic, his weight shifted toward his hind end—spoke volumes about his emotional state. Zack wasn't being disobedient at all. The poor dog was frightened! I described what Zack's body language meant and Tony's face fell.

"I had no idea. I feel *terrible!* I've been forcing him to come here for weeks during rush hour, when the whole world seems to be passing through this plaza. I thought he'd snap out of it. It must have been torture for him!"

It's easy to misunderstand canine body language. Zack certainly looked like a typical out-of-control dog that day in the plaza. Imagine the potential bond damage that could have occurred, though, if Tony had decided to punish Zack for his "disobedience." Poor Zack was acting strangely because of fear, and to scold him or punish him while he was in such distress would have made the problem worse and done some major damage to their bond. That's why learning to understand what your dog is saying is so critically important. Miscommunication can be a *major* bond destroyer.

You probably know more about canine posture than you realize. You meet an unleashed dog during a jog and you can tell that she might be a threat. How? She's standing tall and walking with confidence. She approaches you without hesitation. Her whole body—head, chest, feet—is oriented toward you. Because you're in a potentially dangerous situation, you're speaking dog like a pro. It's now time to apply that same power of observation to your own a dog. Don't let your internal dialogue with your dog ("I know she's mad at me") cloud what she's actually saying to you with her body.

Head

A dog's body will usually clue you in to her emotional "big picture," while the various parts of the head will help you fine-tune exactly how she's feeling. The ears, eyes, forehead, and muzzle all work together to provide a snapshot of canine emotion. Some of the head-based language is incredibly subtle, so don't be frustrated if the nuances of a forehead wrinkle or tongue flick are lost on you at first. Coat color, facial features, and ear type can also affect the clarity of the message being sent. Picture the difference between a German Shepherd's stand-up ears and a Cocker Spaniel's long, floppy ears, and you'll understand what I mean!

The canine body parts work together to communicate emotion, so it's difficult to look at just one part to determine a dog's emotional state. People run into trouble when they focus on one body part, like the person who says, "That dog was wagging her tail and then she bit me!" That said, I'm going to do exactly what I just told you *not* to do and isolate some of my canine clients' most memorable head-based nonverbal cues.

Ears

I can't think about ears without thinking about Juniper. Nervous Juniper always kept her ears plastered to her head during our lessons. She was an Elkhound mix who never learned to accept guests in her home, so even though she came to like me as training progressed, she always opted to sit a few steps away from me and keep her triangle ears tucked close to her head for most of my visits. If I sat and chatted with her owners prior to the lesson, her ears would gradually relax and revert to their natural state, but the moment I moved, they'd flip right back down. I think that dogs can "smile" with their ears, and I didn't get to see Juniper's smiling ears as often as I would have liked during our lessons. Her constantly flattened ears told me that no matter how many times I showed up on her doorstep, she would always be anxious in my presence.

Hank was a young German Shepherd mix whose ears looked two sizes too big for his head. They were the most expressive ears I'd ever encountered. They swiveled, they flopped, they flattened, and they flared. Hank lived in the city and was having a tough time adjusting to the constant noise just outside his building. During our walks, his ears seemed like they were doing push-ups on his head. Was that a jackhammer? Ears tucked. ("Ooooh, that sound makes me nervous!") A barking dog in the distance? Ears pricked. ("You've got my attention, wherever you are!") A crying baby? Ears flattened so they came out the sides of his head. ("I'm not sure *what* that is, but it sounds strange.") When we hit the rare quiet patch of street, his ears rested and only swiveled to listen to our conversation above him. His giant ears, though ungainly, telegraphed much of what was going on inside his head. They were like the CliffsNotes of his emotional state.

Some dogs are handicapped in the ear department due to cropping. Many breeds with naturally floppy ears—such as Boxers, Dobermans, and Great Danes—have their ears *cropped,* or surgically altered so that they stand up to conform to the breed standard. Ear cropping and *tail docking* (surgically removing most of the tail) were historically defended for reasons of hygiene and safety while working in the field, but the practices have come under fire in the past decade. The procedures, often on puppies as young as 9 weeks of age, have been likened to cosmetic surgery on unwilling patients. Additionally, cropping and docking can affect the normal tail and ear communication that goes on between dogs. Many countries have banned the practice. Sadly, it's still legal in the United States. My own Sumner had his ears done before we brought him into our home, and eight years later we still ponder how much cuter and more expressive he'd be with natural, floppy ears.

The dog on the left has natural ears, while Sumner (on the right) has cropped ears.

Forehead

It's a good thing dogs haven't discovered Botox, because their wrinkly fore-heads can convey a great deal of information. Chloe was a yellow Lab/Chow mix whose expressive forehead spoke volumes about her emotional state. Loud noises and fast movement sent her over the edge, so I did my best to tone down my naturally booming voice and spastic gesturing at our first les-son. The training gods were conspiring against me, though, and I knocked over my heavy equipment bag just moments after sitting down for our Q&A. It didn't make a very loud thump as it hit the floor, but it was loud enough to make Chloe pick her head up off the carpet with her forehead wrinkled in concern.

"Oh my," she seemed to say, "What was *that?* Should I run?"

The "I'm nervous and alert" forehead wrinkle is a fairly subtle emotional signal that can be further hindered by coat color—for example, Sumner's brindle pattern and blaze on his forehead camouflage his worry wrinkles—and, depending on the breed, "character" wrinkles can further hinder the forehead messaging. The typical English Bulldog has forehead wrinkles twenty-four hours a day!

Eyes

I'll admit it: It's not always easy to read a dog's eyes. Most dog body lan-guage is fleeting, and that's particularly true of the information conveyed by those nickel-size windows into the canine soul. You might have heard that it's not a good idea to stare directly into a dog's eyes, and while that's fine advice when you don't know the dog before you, there's absolutely nothing wrong with gazing into your dog's limpid pools now and again. You'll find some valuable emotional cues in them.

The first time I met Dane, a creatively named Great Dane, I knew some-thing was off about him. He was only 11 weeks old, but he didn't exhibit any of the typical puppy behaviors I normally see. He kept his distance from me at first, and he didn't appear interested in the toys and bones I'd brought along. Despite our slow start, his first training session went well. At the end of the lesson, when I sat down to discuss homework with his owner, Dane felt comfortable enough to stay in the same room with us and work on the bully bone I'd given him.

When it came time for me to collect my "library bone" (you can borrow it but you can't keep it!), I didn't even think to offer Dane a trade in exchange for it. Instead, I swooped in, not really paying attention to Dane and still chat-ting with his owner as I moved toward him. As I got closer to him, the look he gave me stopped me cold.

Mine!

So how did I get my bone back from Dane without ending up in the emergency room? Instead of continuing toward him and risking a confrontation, I reached into my pocket and then dropped a handful of treats on the ground a few steps away from where he was sitting with the bone. I quickly retrieved it when he got up to collect the scattered treats, and then I had a serious conversation with Dane's owner about Dane's guarding behavior.

If your dog is exhibiting resource guarding behavior, don't punish him to "show him who's boss"—that'll only exacerbate the problem. Find an experienced dog-friendly trainer to assist you in dealing with the issue.

Dane stared at me, unblinking, silent, and completely still. His eyes looked hard. I didn't even have to look at his ears, forehead, or muzzle to understand what he was trying to say to me. Those eyes made it clear: "Don't even think of it, sister. Not. Your. Bone." I was chilled that a dog so young could convey a message with such devastating clarity. I'll never forget that look.

A common eye communication that's on the opposite side of the spectrum from Dane's hard stare is half-moon eye: The white part of the inner eyelid is visible in the corners of the eyes, indicating fearfulness. Think about how your dog looks as she's peering over her shoulder at the vet taking her temperature. Her eyes are probably wide and almost bulging (though my Zeke's eyes *always* look like that!), and there's that telltale ring of white along the border. Half-moon eye typically indicates a dog in distress.

Luckily, I can only recall a handful of times when I've spotted half-moon eye in a canine client. No matter how fearful the dog I'm working with, my goal is to keep our sessions stress free so that the nervous dog is able to process the information. (Sasha, the poor car-reactive Rhodesian Ridgeback in chapter 1, was an exception.) When my clients say, "Want to see how she looks when she's scared? All I have to do is pull out the ironing board!" I tell them no thanks—there's no reason to compound the fear in an already fearful dog. Because of that, my half-moon eye sightings are rare.

Muzzle and mouth

Learning to read your dog's mouth area goes well beyond biting and growling. If you wait for those indicators, it's likely you've missed a few volumes worth of communication! The muzzle—including the mouth *carriage* (the way the mouth is held), the lips, and the tongue—all provide additional commentary on your dog's state of mind.

Winthrop the Greyhound greeted me happily at the front door. After a long run working with shy dogs, I was pleased to be training an outgoing Greyhound. His owners and I settled in to do our Q&A, while Winthrop sat nearby, munching on a bone I'd brought. We glanced over at him frequently as we chatted. "Does Winthrop do this?" "Oh no, Winthrop does that." "Tell me about Winthrop's this and that." Talk, glance, talk, glance. He seemed to take note of the name-dropping and intense attention. It was as if he could tell something was about to go down. After a short time, I saw that Winthrop had stopped chewing the bone. He began panting heavily, as if he'd been running. The bone sat undisturbed between his front feet.

"Uh-oh," I thought. "Maybe I misjudged that initial greeting."

We set to work on the easy introductory exercises, and the panting grew more exaggerated. Winthrop's mouth was wide open and tense. The panting would have seemed normal had he just come off the track, but the fact was, we'd barely moved five steps around the small room while working on the foundation for coming when called. Though our introductory lesson was fun and easy, it only took a few repetitions before Winthrop decided that he was done for the day. He plopped into a down position and simply refused to move. I wholeheartedly agreed with his decision—the guy was cooked. It became clear to me that his initial good cheer at the front door was actually tinged with stress, but I was too busy greeting his owners to take note. Performance anxiety, nerves, fear—whatever he was feeling during that first lesson manifested in his nonstop panting.

Panting is one of those easy-to-overlook communicators because it's ubiquitous—dogs do it all the time. The secret to understanding if there's more to your dog's pant is to look at the context. In Winthrop's case, it was clear that the panting was in no way related to an exertion of energy—the guy hadn't moved from his bed for the entire twenty minutes we sat and chatted about him! The next week, his owners told me that they caught Winthrop panting in a few other nonexercise scenarios (like the first time they tried to take him downstairs to the basement), and because they recognized the behavior as stress related, they took the necessary steps to calm him down.

The tongue provides additional discourse. Lizard tongue is something I frequently see in small dogs, and my client Benny the Chihuahua was no exception. He was a friendly, happy little guy, *until* I tried taking photos of him. I frequently photograph my canine students for my blog, and Benny— with his bejeweled collar and big-dog attitude—was a prime candidate for Internet fame. I got on my belly and began snapping away. Benny's attitude immediately morphed from "Hey, world, check me out!" to "Mommy, please get that flashing monster away from me!" He turned away from the camera. When he had the courage to turn back to face me, his little tongue flicked out of his mouth repeatedly. He would look away, and then look back at me and lick-lick-lick in an attempt to telegraph his discomfort. The few photos I managed to snap of him on that day made him look like he'd been eating onion-flavored ice cream. His stress over being a supermodel was clear in the images.

This dog is panting because she just finished playing a rigorous game. There's no stress in her pant—she looks like she's smiling!

Licking is the cousin to lizard tongue—it's another tongue-based communicator that often goes unnoticed as a potential stress signal. My own Zeke is a champion stress licker. He recently spent time with my young niece and found her relentless affection during a game of fetch overwhelming. She repeatedly offered him the ball, hovered near his face, and did everything in her power to reengage his tired old bones in yet another round of the game. He responded by repeatedly licking her each time she crowded him.

"He likes me! He's kissing me!" she squealed.

I broke it to her gently that Zeke was, in fact, trying to get her to leave him alone. The nonstop licking was his way of saying, "Please go away, little person. I'd like a break." His licking had historically made people back away from him—it's anything but cute—and because the behavior was unintentionally reinforced, Zeke kept it in his repertoire. It works for him. He licks, and people back off. Many dogs lick when they're nervous or aroused by activity, like my client Snowball the Poodle. Every time I saw her, she'd go into a licking frenzy, sloppily attacking every exposed area of skin.

Licking is contextual, though. It can be an indication of an obsessive-compulsive behavior. If the licking is repetitive, trancelike, and difficult to interrupt (meaning, you try to get your dog's attention and you can't), it's time to schedule an appointment with your vet for a checkup.

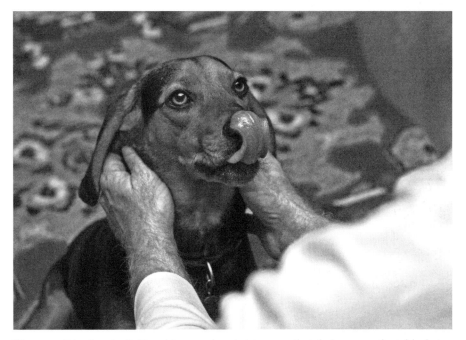

The way this dog is licking his muzzle might mean that he's uncomfortable being touched this way.

Tail

We all know about waggy tails, right? A wagging tail is the most basic, most obvious canine good-mood indicator, right?

Not really.

The potential happiness behind the wag is determined by looking at a number of factors, including tail position, the speed of the wag, and the attendant hind-end movements. A wagging tail is just an indication of a willingness to interact, which can mean war *or* peace. Unfortunately, we can't always translate the tail because so many breeds don't have obvious ones. Zeke's poor little tail is a tiny, crooked, piglike affair that doesn't wag so much as creak back and forth.

Guinness the Beagle had a handsome, long tail that helped to signal his moods. He always reacted inhospitably when he saw another dog during his walks, with his tail acting as a stress-level barometer. He spent most of his time outside, scanning the horizon for interlopers, and the moment he spotted one, even blocks away, his tail went straight up and quivered. Left . . . . right. Left. Right. Leftright. His tail movements could easily be misinterpreted as friendly wagging given that his tail was up and moving back and forth (the definition of *wag,* right?), but the emotion behind the high, tight movements was anything but welcoming. Guinness was broadcasting a terse message: "I'm aroused and ready."

Luna the Italian Greyhound had grown up pottying inside the house on pads when she lived in a high-rise apartment, but her owner had recently relocated to a house with a big yard and wanted Luna to take advantage of it. I was with them on a cold winter morning, encouraging Luna to "release her burden" on the frozen grass. The yard was as good as glass shards to the poor, delicate girl. She was used to city sidewalks and narrow plots of overgrown weeds in her old neighborhood, and the vast expanse of green had her stumped. She didn't know what to do! The frigid temperature wasn't helping matters. Her long tail was so cemented between her legs that I doubt she could have eliminated even if she'd wanted to. The combination of her physical discomfort and confusion about why we were all standing around staring at her drew her tail up to her belly as if it were magnetized.

My former client Lilly was a Pug who never let her lack of tail keep her from communicating her happiness. She greeted me each week with a joy so overwhelming that her solid little body turned crescent-shaped from her attempted wagging. The girl's stumpy tail switched back and forth, but it was almost as if she compensated for her lack of obvious tail-wagginess by wagging her entire hind end! A happy wag engages much more than just the tail. A loose, welcoming wag brings the backfield in motion as well, so that the wag seems to extend up the tail bone. There's no mistaking the message behind a wag that includes the rear end and travels all the way down to dancing feet: That's a wag that says, "Hello, friend!"

Feet

I was finishing up a difficult lesson with my clients Courtney and Jason. Their Poodle, Molly, had recently been attacked by an off-leash neighborhood dog, and she was now petrified of leaving her front yard. We had made minor progress that morning, but it was clear that we had a long way to go with Molly. Despite the fact that we had barely nudged Molly out of her comfort zone, she was still exhibiting stress signals.

As we chatted in their front yard—a place where Molly presumably still felt safe—Molly walked back and forth on the driveway. I glanced down at her.

"Oh, wow," I said. "Look at the ground near her feet."

Courtney and Jason both peered down. "Footprints," Jason said. "I can see her footprints on the blacktop."

Sure enough, Molly was leaving sweaty little footprints behind her as she paced. "Let's move the conversation inside. Molly might not be as comfortable in the front as we thought."

Dogs sweat through the pads of their feet, so sweaty paw prints can be expected after vigorous activity, but those sweaty prints can also be an indication of stress. We hadn't exerted much energy that morning, and the weather was mild, so we knew that Molly wasn't sweating due to activity levels or temperature. The poor little dog was still nervous about being outside, despite the fact that we were safely ensconced in her front yard behind a white picket fence.

Back in the early days of my training career, when I was still trapped in Choke-chain-ville, I attempted a controversial training technique on Sumner. I had heard that flooding was an appropriate technique to deal with

---

A risky proposition

As Jerry Seinfeld would say, "Who *are* these people?" Who are these people who think that it's okay to allow their dogs to walk unleashed through suburban neighborhoods? It's dangerous for the unleashed dog (one stray squirrel on the other side of the street and you've got a tragedy on your hands), as well as for any other leashed dogs they might run into during the walk.

There's one tony city near my house where unleashed dogs are an epidemic. Walking a dog off-leash in that neighborhood seems to provide some sort of bragging rights for the owner—"Look how well trained my dog is!" The fact is, many of these supposedly well-trained dogs are allowed to rush up and interrogate the leashed dogs they meet, not taking into account that the other dogs might be fearful or aggressive. Are you one of those people? Don't be.

fearfulness, so I decided to give it a try on Sumner to help combat his overall nervousness. I took him to a large chain hardware store and stood in the entry with him, right where all the action occurred. The checkout counter was just a few feet away from us. People of all shapes and sizes passed by, pushing noisy carts loaded with plywood and sheet rock. The PA system crackled above us. Sumner was wild with fear. He panted, trembled, and tried to climb into my lap every time I squatted next to him. I was still a training newbie, so even though I didn't understand what the sweat-painted paw prints around me meant, I had a visceral feeling that they mattered. (The panting and trembling? That was old news.)

Tracking sweaty paws can be tough unless you have the right kind of substrate beneath your dog's feet. They won't register in grass or on carpet. The one place where you're probably sure to see them? The vet's office. Even the best socialized dog can fall prey to fearfulness when faced with rectal thermometers and uncomfortable probing.

Trapped in a flood

Flooding is a behavioral desensitization program for treating phobias and fearfulness in which anxiety-producing stimuli are presented at a high intensity and continued until the fear response is diminished. For example, if you're afraid of clowns, your treatment plan might involve locking yourself in a room full of clowns until you've calmed down enough to realize that they can't harm you.

The technique is less effective for dogs than other behavioral-modification programs like systematic desensitization, which decreases the phobic response though gradual exposure to the anxiety-producing stimulus. Treating clown phobia through systematic desensitization might involve presenting a single clown at a great distance away, and, as your fear decreases, gradually moving it closer.

Flooding has experienced an unfortunate resurgence in popularity due to television shows demonstrating the technique on dogs.

Chapter 4

PRIVILEGES VS. RIGHTS

We owe our dogs a set list of unquestionable rights. They include the obvious essentials like food, shelter, proper healthcare, and comfort, as well as often overlooked rights like exercise, training, and companionship. We run into trouble when we provide certain privileges along with those rights. Rights are essential for survival. Deny them and Animal Control might come knocking on your door. Privileges are the things that make life fun for your dog (and for you!), like accompanying you to the farmer's market or running around off-leash. Unfortunately, many people grant privileges before their dog is actually ready for them, which invites frustration into the relationship and chips away at the bond. Many of the calls I receive are from people who've mistakenly granted privileges before their dogs were ready, and now they need my help reversing the damage. To keep your bond as frustration-free as possible, privileges must be worked toward, and you and your dog have to earn them as a team.

Creating a set of boundaries for your dog and working with him to help him earn additional privileges establish you as the benevolent and unquestionable leader in the household. (Notice that I didn't say "alpha"!) It also keeps you honest about your relationship with your dog. Did you take the time to teach your dog how to greet people at the front door, or do you just let him have at them with an apologetic shrug? Is he responsive enough to politely accompany you on your errands around town, or do you just ignore his pulling and barking? Our dogs are only as good as we allow them to be.

Privilege #1: Full Household Freedom

I'm always floored when I get a call from someone complaining that her dog has been urinating in her bedroom for three years, or destroying every new pair of shoes that walks through the door. I refrain from asking the simple question "Why is that?" because I know the answer will have something to do with the dog's desire to retaliate for perceived wrongs or unquenchable chewing habit. The truth is that the dog has probably been granted more freedom than he's actually earned.

Most people understand that new dogs need to live in a puppy-proofed environment until they're reliably housetrained (at least two consecutive months without an accident in the house) and chew-trained (they can be trusted not to chew on inappropriate household items). Problems arise when the dog physically matures out of puppyhood and *looks* like an adult but hasn't actually graduated out of puppy status due to repeated accidents ("He only pooped in the house twice this week") or unchecked household destruction ("He made that hole in the bedspread bigger last night"). Just because your dog *looks* like he's grown up doesn't mean that he actually is.

I want to be clear, though. I am in no way placing the blame on your dog for household accidents and chewing. Teaching your dog the rules of housetraining and chew training is 100 percent up to you. If you don't take the time to teach your dog where to potty and what to chew, how will he learn? It's up to you to set up your dog to succeed by managing his world, and helping him to understand how to live in ours. Unlike some of the other team-based privileges, where you and your dog work and train together to earn the privilege, attaining this reward rests squarely on your shoulders.

Maggie called me in a panic. Her Yorkie, Cassidy, had been urinating in her large walk-in closet for over a year, and the behavior had to be stopped.

"Why now? What changed?" I asked. (This is my standard question for someone looking to immediately end a long-term problem.)

"My boyfriend just invited me to vacation with his family at their house in Martha's Vineyard. They said I can bring Cassidy, but they don't know about her peeing problem. And I don't think his mom likes dogs very much."

I rolled my eyes. I'm not a fan of eleventh-hour training assignments, but I agreed to meet with her.

Maggie turned out to be a kind, earnest dog owner. It was clear that she adored Cassidy but didn't know what to do about the closet problem. Maggie faced the typical toy dog challenge in that Cassidy's messes were silver-dollar

A shoe is a shoe is a shoe

Despite what it might seem like, your dog does not target your most valuable shoes or sunglasses, and he doesn't eliminate in the house because he's "mad" at you for going back to work on Monday. Dogs have a variety of nuanced emotions, certainly, but they lack an understanding of our material goods. (four hundred dollars at Nordstrom or $25 at Payless? It doesn't matter to dogs—both pairs smell like feet.) They don't have complex social emotions like retaliatory anger and timed reprisals.

sized, and each one didn't seem like the end of the world. It wasn't like Cassidy was a Mastiff letting loose in the closet! I tried to figure out just what we were facing.

"Have you taken her to a vet to make sure she's healthy?"

"Yes, she's totally fine."

"How long has she been peeing in your closet?"

"Um, forever? No, she's done it pretty much since I brought her home."

"How old is she?"

"A year and a half."

"How many times a week does she do it?"

"At least four times a week. And I'm not even sure I catch all of the messes. Sometimes she hits my dirty laundry on the floor, and there's a chance that I just throw it in the wash and don't even realize it. It just seems like her accidents are nonstop. I can't take it—it's driving me crazy! I think she gets mad at me for leaving her alone, and the pee is her way of getting back at me."

I ignored her last comment. "Does she pee anywhere else in the house?"

Maggie looked sheepish. "Yes, she also pees in my home office. And sometimes on the rug in the front hall. And the family room. Pretty much anyplace where there's carpet."

"So, your home is basically one big toilet, right?"

"Yeah, I guess it is."

The more I probed, the more obvious it became that Maggie had made a halfhearted attempt at potty training Cassidy when she was a puppy but didn't stick with it. Maggie started off with all the necessary potty-training tools—an appropriately sized crate, numerous baby gates, an odor-eliminating cleaning solution for slipups, and, most important, keen supervision. But after two glorious accident-free weeks, when Cassidy was 16 weeks old, Maggie assumed that her dog had graduated Potty Training 101. Maggie prematurely transitioned Cassidy off the training aides and granted her unfettered access to her entire apartment.

When I pointed this out to Maggie, she seemed relieved to hear that her dog wasn't acting on vindictive impulses. I explained that household freedom should only come after a dog has gone two months without an accident. Maggie's eyes got wide.

"I'm leaving for vacation next week! What am I going to do?"

All was not lost for Maggie and Cassidy. Though Maggie wouldn't be able to completely housetrain her dog in a week, we could take steps to jump-start the process. It turned out that Cassidy didn't mind being in her travel crate, so we worked out a schedule that included crate time when Maggie was at work or home but occupied and unable to watch Cassidy. Maggie invested in a black light and did her best to find and treat the old potty stains so that Cassidy wouldn't be tempted to revisit them. I also suggested that she go back to rewarding Cassidy with an extra-special treat each time she successfully eliminated outside. "You're not rewarding the *act* of elimination, because that already feels good," I told her. "You're rewarding the *location*."

Most important, Maggie agreed to cut off Cassidy's free reign of the house. We reintroduced the baby gates so that Cassidy had a smaller "strike zone" when she was hanging out with Maggie during supervised time. If Maggie couldn't keep a close eye on Cassidy when she was home, she had to put Cassidy in her crate.

"So what do I do at the Vineyard house? This is the first time I'm meeting his parents, and I don't want Cassidy's peeing to make them hate me!"

"Keep working the program," I replied. "You'll have her crate with you, so use that. Take her out frequently, and keep rewarding her for pottying outside. You can't bring baby gates, but you can use your suitcase to block a doorway if necessary. Better yet, use a houseline, a thin, 6-foot leash that you put her on and attach to your waist. That way she can't dash out of sight and pee. If your future in-laws—fingers crossed!—ask you why you're wearing your dog, just shrug it off and say that their house is lovely and you want to make sure that Cassidy minds her manners. It won't be easy next week, but you can make it happen."

Maggie e-mailed me three weeks later. Cassidy had had only two accidents in the Vineyard house, which she cleaned before anyone found out. Her at-home housetraining plan was proving to be difficult, but it was working. Maggie missed the freedom of letting Cassidy roam the house, but she realized that the Big Brother approach was a means to an end. She could see progress. The best news was that her boyfriend's mother adored Cassidy and decided that she wanted a Yorkie, too!

Though full household access feels like a right—you want your dog to have freedom and comfort—until you've helped your dog to learn the house rules, it's a privilege. Granting your dog the run of the house before he's actually earned it is guaranteed to lead to frustration. Without gentle instruction and guidance from you, Fido won't understand that he's not supposed to pee in the guest room or use the couch pillows as chew toys. Invest the time to make sure that your dog is ready for the privilege of full household access, and you'll never be faced with a bond-damaging surprise.

Privilege #2: Access to Guests

I've worked with quite a few people who've told me that their dog's behavior is an embarrassment when they have guests over. The barking, jumping, and pestering make them dread hosting special occasions. When they try to lock Fido away in Bedroom Siberia, he yodels his displeasure for the entire time, so they have no choice but to keep him out and allow his misbehavior with an apologetic shrug. Meanwhile, Aunt Jane gets covered in saliva and muddy paw prints, and Uncle Frank deals with appetizer theft.

Access to guests is a privilege that *must* be earned because there are so many opportunities for your dog to reward himself for inappropriate behavior while you're busy hosting the event. That stolen egg roll? It tasted great, it was easy to acquire, and your dog just spotted your 6-year-old nephew passing by with a plate full of them. One quick swipe and that behavior will be rewarded for a second time in a short period. Your guests are probably too polite to complain when he relentlessly paws at them for petting, so they eventually give in and essentially teach him that persistence pays off. The dog who pesters the most wins! Every behavior that is rewarded, even accidentally, is reinforced and made stronger, so all those "little slipups" can combine to create one beastly, inhospitable dog.

Welcome to the dreaded catch-22 of privileges: How do you help your dog to earn the privilege of hanging out with guests if he acts like a lunatic every time you have guests over? Practice, of course.

You first have to find a few willing "victims" who understand that they're offering up their body parts for the greater good and won't mind the occasional canine misstep like jumping or barking. It's best to start with the behavior that sets the tone for the rest of your dog's guest drama: his front-door greetings.

Instead of sequestering your dog away when the doorbell rings (which does little but bottle his energy until he's finally released to pounce on the guest), it's most effective to address the behavior right at the source. Nearly all my clients want help with their dog's jumpy front-door greetings, and I warn each and every one of them that it's an extremely difficult behavior to change. It probably has a long reinforcement history—your dog received lots of positive attention when he jumped on people as a puppy because it was cute, and the behavior still gets attention from you and guests, whether positive or negative); it's highly rewarding to the dog (it feels *good* to connect with new people—those paws on your thighs are the canine equivalent of a handshake). Finally, if you're like me, you have guests infrequently so you can't practice with your dog very often. When you're welcoming company into your home, the last thing you want to think about is dog training!

If your dog is a larger breed that elicits shrieks of pain when he lands his jumps, begin working on this behavior using a tether, a thin but sturdy four- to six-foot nylon or cotton leash that gets anchored to a doorknob, stair post, or heavy piece of furniture close to the front door. Fido gets attached to the other end with enough slack in the leash so that he can range a few steps in each direction, but not so much slack that he can join you right at the front door.

The grumpy dog trainer

I can tolerate most canine misbehavior, but getting jumped on really bothers me. It's painful! In the summertime, when the heat forces me to wear shorts, my legs end up scratched and bruised. I refuse to sweat it out in jeans, so I've improvised an option that keeps me somewhat protected and isn't too hot: I wear a thick groomer's apron over my shorts. I always put it on before I walk into a new client's home (which is when I get jumped on the most). I'm sure that I present quite a picture in my long blue plastic "skirt."

Tethering is a great way to teach your dog how to greet guests without allowing him to get close enough to jump up on them.

It's best to buy a spare leash to use as your tether so that you can leave it in place after you're done with it. Invite your victim into the house *without* having her knock or ring the doorbell first. Act as you normally would when welcoming a guest. Smile, hug, chat, and do your best to ignore the quivering mass of fur just four steps away from you. After the greeting, walk with your guest toward your dog on his tether, both of you assuming the arm-cross sit.

Your dog will probably jump up and dance around before he's able to make the connection between you and your guest's crossed arms and what they actually mean. Stand a short distance away from him until he's able to settle into a sit, toss a treat near his feet, and then walk toward him with your guest. The tossed treat is essentially a reset button that allows your dog to get rewarded for performing the sit, burn off a tiny bit of energy when he gets up to collect the treat, and then hopefully go right back into the sit as you approach with your arms crossed.

If your dog starts jumping again, turn your back to him and walk away. You're now tapping into the "attract/repel" theory of dog training. When he does something you like (sitting), he attracts you to him. When does something you *don't* like, jumping, he repels you away from him. Repeat the process until he can maintain the sit until you and your guest are right in front of him, at which time you can deliver a treat and allow your guest to touch and interact with him. If he resumes jumping and acting overeager, go back to your attract/repel scenario.

The arm-cross sit

The arm-cross sit is a nonverbal sit cue, and my favorite way to deal with jumpy greeting behavior. Your dog learns that when you do a very clear nonverbal signal—crossing your arms—it means that he should sit.

To teach it, grab a few treats and a hungry pooch. Walk across the room with your dog, come to a stop, cross your arms across your chest, and look at your dog. He'll probably stand there looking back at you for a few moments, and then plop into a sit (particularly if he knows that you have treats in your pocket!). Click the moment he sits, or mark the behavior by using a word like "Yup!" or "Good!" Repeat the process, clicking or saying "Yup" right as his bum hits the ground.

There's no need to say "Sit" to your dog—with enough repetitions, the very obvious arm-cross alone will do the trick. Dogs actually learn nonverbal cues more easily than verbal ones. Get all of your family members and friends to try the arm-cross with your dog as well so that he begins to generalize the behavior. It's a cool little cue! Plus, it's an effective way of dealing with jumpy greeting behavior because it's more obvious than a verbal cue (dogs' ears tend to fuse shut when they're overly excited), and it keeps your guests from engaging in accidental touching, petting, or shooing away that might encourage more jumping.

The arm-cross sit is my favorite training trick.

Repeat the entire sequence several times with different guests until your dog recognizes the arm-cross sit and automatically goes into a sit when he sees someone doing it near the front door. He doesn't have to hold a sit the entire time you're opening the door and welcoming your guest (that's really, really hard, graduate-level work), but he should assume a sit as soon as you and your guest go into the arm-cross sit.

Now that you've made it through the basics, add a new dose of reality: have your victim ring the doorbell! Pavlov was on to something with that bell idea—you'll find your dog will react as if you never practiced at all. Doorbells and knocks are so deeply conditioned to mean excitement at the front door that even if Fido sees the same victim he's been greeting at the door after hearing the bell, he's likely to respond as if he hasn't seen the person in weeks. Begin doing surprise drills and have members of your family ring the bell or knock each time they come home, so that your dog begins to realize that ringing and knocking don't always mean fresh meat. Eventually, if you practice enough, you'll be able to transition off of the tether and allow your dog to stand near you at the door when you welcome guests. Keep in mind, though, that this behavior can be incredibly difficult to change given the scarcity of guests and your dog's long reward history.

Once you've passed the first guest hurdle, it's on to the rest of the party. Make sure your dog is proficient with his basic obedience skills like stay and bed when it's just you and your family home, and then introduce the skills while your patient victims are helping out. (Need some help polishing up your dog's basic obedience? Check out chapter 5.) Practice bed when you're standing together in the kitchen. Then give it a shot when you're sitting at the dining room table or on the couch. Instruct your guests to avoid your dog's attempts at conversation with them until he's safely ensconced on the bed. You want him to understand that going to his bed attracts people to him like a magnet . . . *everyone* wants to have an audience with the prince on his pillow! Try working on stays in the kitchen as you serve coffee. Think of as many different party scenarios as possible and help him learn how to react to them.

Training or management

You always have two options when it comes to dog behavior problems: training or management. Training is teaching your dog a behavior that he can perform instead of engaging in the problem behavior, like getting him to hold a stay while you clean up the spilled beer from the floor instead of the two of you wrestling over the puddle. Management is putting your dog in a scenario where the inappropriate behavior can't take place at all, like keeping your dog in the bedroom when the pizza man shows up to keep him from going nuts at the front door. Management doesn't actually change the problem behavior—your dog probably still wants to attack the delivery man—but it's a quick, easy way to address the issue when training isn't an option.

This puppy is learning to love his activity toy.

There are many management steps you can take to enable your dog to hang out with you when you have guests. Tiring him out with play before people arrive is an obvious help. Keeping him busy with a special activity toy while your friends mix and mingle will further dilute his drive to entertain the masses. Not so long ago there was only one treat stuffing toy available for dogs, the mighty Kong. Now, there are so many that I couldn't begin to list them all.

It's best to identify your dog's favorite toy type before you test it out on him during an event. Does he prefer the kind he can move around the room to get it to dispense treats? Is he a super-chewer who can only be trusted with the sturdiest of treat-dispensing toys? Will he get frustrated and give up if the payoff takes too long?

Once you've identified the toy type, consider what you're going to put in it, and how you're going to secure the goods inside the toy. The common complaint I hear is, "My dog is finished with treat toys within five minutes, and then he's back to pestering everyone." Typically, the Quick-Draw McGraw dog is only tasked with cleaning out a few tablespoons of peanut butter. Too easy! Get creative when you stuff the toy. Try peanut butter, layer some soft banana on top of the peanut butter, add a row of cereal (like Cheerios), and then seal off the top with a flat dog biscuit. Or fill the toy with chicken broth, stabilize it in a drinking glass and then freeze it to make a

Tying an activity toy to a chair is a great way to keep your dog busy and anchored to one area of the house.

dogsicle (although this can be messy). Most treat-dispensing toys have holes in them, so you can feed a sturdy piece of string through one of the holes and anchor it to a chair leg so that he has to stay in one area to enjoy it.

Make sure that your dog is comfortable with people coming near him when he has a high-value chew toy. You don't want the well-intentioned pat on the head to turn into a bite.

It's important that your guests understand that you're working with your dog to improve his manners. Every family has the dog lover who says, "It's okay, let him jump on me! I love dogs!" But every welcomed jump and every rewarded pester cements the behavior in your dog's repertoire. It's not easy to be the dog cop, but it's necessary if you want to clean up his party manners.

Stuff it!

Ten things you probably never realized that you can stuff in your dog's activity toy:

- Banana
- Dog food
- Sliced cheese
- Apples
- Yogurt
- Croutons
- Sour cream
- Cheese in a can
- Carrots
- Lunch meat

I deal with an "untrainer" in my own household: my father insists on feeding Sumner from the table when he visits, and he asks Sumner to jump up and hug him and invites him halfway up on the sofa. Every time my father encourages one of these undesirable behaviors, I harrumph and he looks at me with big eyes and a "What did I do?" look. Luckily, Summie knows that the naughty behaviors are only allowed when my parents are visiting.

Helping your dog to earn the privilege of hanging out with company takes time and dedication. The reason unmannerly behavior is rampant in dogs is that the behavior is so challenging to address. Unfortunately, we have limited opportunities to invite understanding friends and family into the house to work on training. A plan that includes a combination of training and management will eventually get Fido to the point where he's a welcoming canine ambassador in your home.

Privilege #3: Field Trips

We all want to take our dogs on the road. It's fun to sit outside the coffee shop with your dog resting at your feet and let strangers coo over how adorable he is. Unfortunately, the reality is more often a long way from that idyllic vision. Sketchy leash manners, an inability to settle down, and a drive to greet every passerby can turn the dream into a nightmare. Field trips are yet another privilege that your dog must earn with your help through training and polite behavior.

I met Seamus and his person for the first time in the pet supply store parking lot. It was a Saturday afternoon, and the place was packed with people and dogs. I could see Seamus bounding from front seat to back seat, over and over again, as I approached their car, barking and pushing his nose up against the glass. His owner, Carol, stood outside shaking her head.

"Wow," I said. "He looks . . . excited!"

"You ain't seen nothing," she said with a half-grin, half-smirk.

She slowly cracked the car door keeping her body braced against it, and Seamus shoved his big blocky Lab head through the opening. He leaned his weight on the door, and it flew open as if it were made of cardboard. Carol managed to grab his collar as he slipped by, preventing him from taking off across the parking lot. She wrestled him for a few moments, trying to attach his leash while he did everything in his power to make friends with a Corgi passing by.

Once leashed, Seamus pulled full-tilt toward the pet-store doorway. It was clear he'd been there before and knew what awaited him inside. He barreled to the counter, hopped up, and demanded a treat from the clerk, which she dutifully provided with a smile. Then, still chewing, Seamus tore off after a Bichon puppy just rounding the corner. Carol had no choice but to follow behind him—he outweighed her by a few pounds—and she smiled as he poked his big nose into the supine puppy's belly. A woman passed by and said, "Aw, how cute." Seamus took her compliment as an invitation and jumped up on her, pushing her back slightly. He then realized that he was mere steps away from the chew aisle, so he yanked his way over to the massive bones displayed on the lowest shelf.

"You want that one, huh?" Carol said as Seamus helped himself.

Meanwhile, I tried to cover the logo on my shirt lest any of the other customers think that this plundering pooch was one of my students. Carol had contacted me because she wanted to continue to bring Seamus with her during her errands, but she realized that the behavior he got away with as a puppy was no longer manageable now that he was an adolescent.

Based on what I saw that morning, it was clear to me that Carol had done a lovely job socializing her dog—Seamus was very sweet-tempered—but she had handed over the privilege of accompanying her on frequent field trips without helping him to earn it. Socialization in a puppy is a *requirement,* but tagging along with Carol on her errands every day was something that Seamus needed to work toward and earn with repeated good behavior. Carol lived in a very dog-friendly town, so she could take Seamus with her to the dry cleaner's, the bank, the farmer's market, and various outdoor cafes. But just because she *could* didn't mean that she *should.* Seamus's over-the-top performance that day helped me illustrate to Carol that he wasn't ready for the incredibly fun privilege she was offering him.

My next appointment with Carol and Seamus took place early on a Monday morning in a deserted, unfamiliar shopping plaza down the street from the pet store. We started off with Seamus's car manners. He did his usual seat hurdling prior to being let out of the car, but instead of opening the door for him mid-jump as she usually did, Carol waited until Seamus paused for a moment. His face seemed to say, "This is *very* different. What's going on?"

Carol praised him as she slowly opened the car door, her eyebrows rising in shock as he stood there with that same questioning look on his face. "It can't be this easy," she muttered. It wasn't. Seamus snapped out of his reverie when the door hit the midway point and attempted to jump past Carol.

"Shut the door!" I shouted.

Take it on the road

Socialization is the process of introducing your puppy to new experiences in a positive way, so that he learns that the world is a great big fun place. Gentle exposure to new people, places, sounds, and experiences will help build your puppy's confidence. Socialization is one of the most critical steps in puppy development.

Carol and I had mapped out our car strategy beforehand. The idea was that Seamus had to remain calm while Carol opened the door all the way and took hold of his leash (which she had put on him before she got out of her seat) and had to wait until she said "Let's go!" before he exited the car. He was off to a decent start, but I had a feeling that we were going to have an impulse-control issue once the door was open wide and sweet freedom was just inches away.

I was right. Seamus could keep it together until the door was nearly halfway open, but the moment it yawned beyond the halfway point, he bolted. Carol knew that each time Seamus forged ahead she was to shut the door quickly so that he couldn't slip out and have his pushiness rewarded. Because Carol's reflexes were dead-on, it only took four repetitions before Seamus understood that his own actions were delaying his exit. On the fifth attempt, Seamus managed to stand still until the door opened all the way, and though he trembled with excitement the entire time, he waited until Carol reached in, grabbed his leash and said, "Let's go!' before he moved forward.

With that first important step addressed, we set to work on his parking lot leash manners. We had stacked the deck in our favor by arriving at the lot before the rest of the world was even awake. No distracting people or animals to contend with, just unfamiliar terrain and new smells. I asked Carol to visit a variety of parking lots during off-hours until Seamus could navigate all of them politely, and then she was to try an already-conquered lot during a weekday lunch hour when there were more people around. I told her to take Seamus on side visits to dog-friendly stores right as they opened on weekdays so that he had the opportunity to polish up his shopping skills without having to worry about meeting as many new friends.

Only after Seamus had spent a few weeks running the training gauntlet and had successfully practiced his car manners, leash manners, and store manners during off-peak hours did we try to meet in the pet store parking lot on a busy Saturday. I spotted Carol a few rows over from where I parked and I knew that her grin meant that something good was about to go down.

She didn't say a word to me, she just turned to the car where Seamus sat patiently. She opened the door all the way, and he forged ahead slightly because he spotted the Hot Dog Lady just a few feet away, but Carol held up her hand with her palm facing Seamus, as if to say, "Stay there," and he settled back into a trembling but solid sit-stay. She took his leash in her hand, waited a beat, winked at me, and said, "Okay, let's go!" Out he sailed.

After our happy hot-dog-filled reunion, Seamus, Carol, and I headed through the parking lot and into the belly of the beast. Seamus did his very best to match his pace to ours. We entered the store and headed for the counter, where Seamus's favorite checker asked him to sit and then gave him a treat. Then we strolled around the store, and each time Seamus spotted a toy or chew that interested him, Carol asked him to sit, picked the item up, and offered it to him. When a young man asked whether it was okay to pet him, Carol asked him to try the arm-cross sit first. The guy laughed, gave Seamus an ear scratch, and walked away. Seamus beamed.

The differences between my first meeting with Seamus and Carol and our last one were too many to count. It was as if Seamus had matured into a proper gentleman in a matter of a few weeks! The two of them worked together as a team to help Seamus learn the ropes of polite public behavior, thereby earning him the privilege of accompanying Carol on her daily errands. She proudly told me about the compliments she was receiving about his new behavior. Instead of saying, "Uh-oh, Seamus," the vendors at the farmer's market were now saying, "Hey! It's Seamus!"

Not every dog needs to go through the rigorous training program that Seamus faced in order to earn field-trip privileges. I've worked with many dogs who aced their first trip to the shopping plaza, state park, or office. Here are the questions to ask yourself about the feasibility of field trips for your dog:

- Does my dog have good manners in and around my car?
- Can my dog walk politely through a crowded parking lot?
- Can my dog greet new dogs and people without losing his mind?
- Am I embarrassed by the way my dog acts in public?

Taking your dog on the road can be a joy if you've helped him polish up the skills required for real-world adventures, and chapter 5 will get you started. Every time I see a polite dog strolling through a plaza or resting outside a coffee shop, I look at his owner and think, "Nice work!"

Privilege #4: Off-Leash Freedom

Annabelle was a charming Airedale. She aced all her basic training with me, and, because she progressed through my curriculum quickly, we decided to take a trip to the dog park for one of her final lessons. Despite her success in our weekly classes, her owner, Ted, kept relaying his frustration to me about one little problem: She refused to come to him at the dog park. Every week, he and his wife, Lauren, told me how annoying it was to try to collect Annabelle when it was time to go. They usually spent at least fifteen minutes chasing after her when it was time to leave, trying to corner her and cajole her into letting them put the leash on her.

Dog-park indecision

My clients frequently ask me if I think dog parks are a good idea, and I answer them with a resounding "It depends." Dog parks are excellent in theory—a vast, safe area for dogs to play and exercise—but the reality can be far different. Too many inappropriate, poorly mannered dogs find their way into dog parks, leading to bullying, fighting, and injury. Couple the poorly behaved dogs with the misinformed owners who can't discern healthy dog play from inappropriate behavior and you have a recipe for disaster.

Initially I was cocky as we headed into the dog park. "No problem, I can clean this up," I thought to myself. "Annabelle worships me. I'll show them how it's done." Ted took off the leash, and Annabelle ran off after a squatty English Bulldog who was already in the enclosure.

"Okay, this behavior is totally fine," I told them. "Annabelle needs to get the lay of the land and meet everyone here before she circles back to us. When she comes up to you to check in, make sure to give her big love. It's a huge compliment that she opted to choose you over the other dogs in that moment."

Ted laughed and shook his head. "That's probably not going to happen."

"Oh, come on! Of course, it will. The treat lady is here with you today—that's got to count for something."

We made small talk as we watched Annabelle circle from dog to dog, chasing this one, rolling on her back for another. The minutes ticked by, and Annabelle didn't even glance in our direction.

We tried moving farther away from the door to the park lest she think that our position next to it meant that we were about to leave. We walked through the park together waiting for her to notice us, and each time we got within twenty paces of her, even if we weren't looking in her direction, Annabelle dashed to the opposite end of the park.

I talked about what I thought was going on and asked the pointed question that was nagging at me. "I can see how this has been frustrating for you. Have you punished Annabelle after you managed to catch her?"

"Not really. I mean, we've never hit her. But I know that I act really stern with her when I finally get her back on the leash. I might have yelled a little on the way to the car a few times," Ted admitted.

"Yeah, I can't help but get angry. It's ridiculous what I have to do to catch her," Lauren chimed in.

"Have you had to trick her to get the leash on?"

"Tricking her worked a few times, but she caught on to what we were doing. I'd squat down and when she came up to me, I'd grab her. Or if she was near the fence and her back was turned away from me, I'd tackle her. Bringing her to the dog park is really driving both of us crazy. We don't know what to do," Lauren replied.

Bingo. Annabelle's avoidance now made sense. The sad fact was that she'd been tricked and bullied into the behavior she was exhibiting. Unfortunately, her inappropriate behavior was reinforcing itself, because getting chased around the dog park was nothing but a game to her that allowed her to stay longer. Plus, by running away, she put off the scolding that was sure to come once her leash was clipped on. I knew we had work to do.

At around the same time I was dealing with Annabelle, I got a call from a woman named Suzanne who desperately needed help with her terrier mix, Bartleby. "He runs away all the time," she said.

All the time? If a behavior is predictable, it's preventable, so I was at a loss as to why her dog repeatedly ran away. If she *knew* it was going to happen, why didn't she *prevent* it from happening?

Turns out she lived on the edge of an open green space where all the dog people in her neighborhood congregated after work. She and Bartleby joined the crowd most nights. Bartleby enjoyed playing with the other dogs, but if he happened to see something intriguing out of the corner of his eye, like a squirrel or a jogger, he took off after it. No amount of calling could bring him back. Despite the repeated annoyance the behavior presented, and how angry it made her, Suzanne never realized that perhaps Bartleby wasn't ready for off-leash freedom. (Unfenced off-leash freedom is a touchy subject. Even the best-trained dogs can take off in the right circumstances. It's a risk no matter how well you've trained your dog.)

Off-leash freedom is a privilege for both parties, a privilege that needs to be *earned* by both parties. It's clearly a privilege for the dog because he gets to run around at top speed with the wind in his ears. It's a privilege for *people* because it relieves them of some of their leash-walking and game-playing responsibilities. Your dog burns through gallons of energy during a thirty-minute jaunt to the dog park, ends up dog-tired, and all you have to do is stand there and drink your coffee. (Or not. Check chapter 9 for what you're *actually* supposed to be doing at the dog park.) A trip to the dog park is a guarantee of at least a few hours of canine repose.

That said, the privilege of playing off-leash should only be awarded to the dog who comes readily when called and opts to keep his people within sight. On the flip side, the owner can only be granted the privilege of letting her dog play off-leash once she has worked with her dog long enough that the dog responds easily to a recall and the owner doesn't have to resort to trickery to get her dog to come along.

Off-leash freedom is a privilege that you and your dog must earn as a team.

Catch-22 time: How can both parties earn the privilege of off-leash play without actually going off-leash?

First, you have to stop allowing outdoor off-leash play until you've made progress with the basic recall (see chapter 5). You can't permit your dog to continue ignoring the recall while you're trying to change your dog's response to it. Perfect your easy house and yard recalls to the point where he *loves* playing the recall game. Then invest in a twenty- to thirty-foot cotton leash that approximates off-leash freedom. A long leash enables your dog to feel like he has room to run, but it gives you the peace of mind that you can reel him in if necessary. Most dog parks don't allow leashed dogs inside, so find a park that allows leashes (a neighborhood park not meant specifically for dogs should do the trick) so that you can work on recalls first. Allow your dog to explore the area before you begin training, and then try a few simple runaway recalls. Have fun

> ## A runaway hit
>
> A runaway recall is a fun way to get your dog revved up to come to you when you call. Call your dog using your recall word, and the moment he looks at you, take off running in the opposite direction from your dog. Allow your dog to chase after you and then reward him when he catches up with a treat or play.

with it and turn the training into a game so that your dog begins to trust you again. Use a high-value treat to reward your dog, or if he enjoys play, use a tug or a ball as the reward. Be encouraging during the process, and don't slip into your drill sergeant voice! *Remember:* You're "untraining" a prior behavior that has baggage.

Once your dog is reliably coming to you on the long line in a variety of environments, take a trip to the dog park during off-peak hours when there aren't as many people and dogs around. Let your dog wander and explore, and then try a recall. If he comes to you, have a *major* party and praise your dog as if he just completed a marathon. If he reverts back to his "I'm not sure about this" behavior when you call, then you're still not ready for off-leash action. Back to the drawing board. Be honest, though. Was your dog reliably responding to the long line exercises, or were you trying to jump from Dick and Jane to Tolstoy?

When your dog is reliably responding to you on the long line in unfamiliar environments and in the dog park during off-peak hours, you can tempt fate and see what happens during dog-park rush hour. Baggage city. Praise your dog any time he chooses to check in with you. If you notice him running in your direction, stack the deck in your favor and call him *then*. He was on his way anyway, but you can make him think that it was your idea! Again, major praise when he chooses correctly. Try the recall a few times before it's time to go (but not too many times!) so that your dog doesn't only associate the word with leaving. Because you've been incorporating the other bonding tips in this book, it's likely that you'll see increased attentiveness from your dog even when you're not calling him to you. Perhaps you won't even have to use your recall word when it's time to go. Your dog will see you heading for the door and decide that now is a fine time to leave, thank you very much.

A strong recall is the foundation for off-leash freedom. Practice makes perfect!

Part II

HOW TO BUILD THE BOND

Chapter 5

BUILDING BLOCK #1:
TRAINING FOR LIFE

Tune into any competition obedience program and you're likely to think, "Now *those* dogs are bonded!" They sure appear to be, with that unbreakable focus on their handlers and amazing responsiveness. The dogs entered in competition obedience trials might indeed be very bonded to their people, but I maintain that perfect behavior in the show ring doesn't necessarily track to a strong bond. Obedience training is a major component of the bond, and it's an obvious outward sign of a good bond, but it's not the soul of it. That said, I can't say enough about how dog-friendly training can strengthen your relationship with your dog.

My goal for my clients is to help them develop an obedience training language that becomes a part of their everyday lives with their dogs. The basic behaviors like sit, down, stay, and come should be as fluid and natural to their dogs as saying "please" and "thank you" are to us. The sad fact is that, more often than not, once classes have ended, the training skills taught in class are quickly relegated to the back burner and then slowly forgotten. A call from a former client drove that point home in a comical but depressing way.

Albert and his French Bulldog, Zoe, had been an amazing duo during training. I looked forward to seeing them every week because it was obvious that Albert did his homework, and Zoe enjoyed the training process. They were dream students, so I was happy to hear from him again two years after we completed training. A lot had changed for Albert in the ensuing years. A new wife, house, and twin babies were reasons enough to schedule a follow-up session.

"So what are we dealing with today, Albert?" I asked after meeting his family and reconnecting with my old friend Zoe.

"Victoria, I have no idea what to do about this stuff Zoe is pulling! She's still really good at everything we did in class, but this one behavior is driving us nuts."

My mind raced. Was she stealing baby toys? Peeing her displeasure about the tiny human interlopers in her house? Barking out the window at passing dogs?

"Do tell."

"Well, every time I open the front door to get the mail, she runs out to the yard and won't come back in! She doesn't take off running or anything, she just wants to hang out in the sun on the front walk."

I was momentarily stunned. *This* was Zoe's major crazy-making behavior? I was thrilled. What a simple fix!

"Albert, you said that she's still good at all her basic obedience skills, right?"

"Yeah, she's great. Hasn't forgotten a thing."

"Okay, I hope I'm not insulting you by saying this, but why haven't you tried putting her in a down-stay at the front door before you walk out?"

He looked at me blankly for a moment. "I never thought of that."

We gave it a shot and, sure enough, Zoe passed the test. Albert asked her to do a down on the carpet about ten steps away from the doorway, told her to stay, and then walked to the door. She started kicking her back feet when he turned the knob (a dog's back feet always telegraph the intent to get up), but he paused and looked over his shoulder at her and she settled back into a comfortable down. He stepped out to the mailbox hanging just outside the door, pretended to collect the mail and then came back in. Zoe held her stay the whole time.

"Look at that—problem solved!" I grinned at Albert. "You might want to think about revisiting your recalls in the front yard so that if she *does* manage to slip out, she'll come back when you call. Oh, and consider giving her more yard time. Maybe grant her front-yard access as a reward for holding the stay. You could put her leash on before you do the stay, go grab your mail, and then release her to go outside and tie the leash to the handrail on your stairs. Then you can sit out there with her while you go through your mail."

I was thrilled that Zoe's "fix" was so easy to enact but concerned that it hadn't dawned on Albert to use the stay he had learned in class. Though I repeatedly remind my clients how they can use the lessons from class in their everyday lives, there seems to be a disconnect when it comes to using all the cool stuff they've learned.

Using basic obedience cues in real-life scenarios is one of the simplest and most effective ways to strengthen your bond. Speaking a common language through training alleviates confusion and frustration. Don't want your dog to play tug of war with your pant leg every morning when you're getting dressed? Don't yell at her to stop—ask her to hold a down-stay! Prefer that she not flail like a fish out of water when you're putting on her leash? Don't ignore it and put the leash on anyway—ask her to sit! Just like every "I love you" makes a marriage stronger, every thoughtful, well-executed obedience cue can make your bond stronger.

Click to it

Remember: You can use a clicker to mark your dog's behavior when she does the right thing, and then follow up with a treat, or use a marker word like "Good!" or "Yup!" and then give her a treat to let her know she nailed it. It can take anywhere from ten to twenty repetitions before your dog makes the connection between the sound of the click or your marker word and the treat about to be delivered.

Even though this book isn't a training primer (the book shelves are groaning with them already), I do want to briefly cover some useful obedience cues and explain how you can incorporate them into your everyday life. Let's begin with my favorite.

Down-Stay

I'm peculiar about stays because I basically ignore sit-stay. I'm not suggesting that it doesn't have its place in the dog-training world—I just think that the down-stay has more applications in everyday life. Though it's quicker to get a dog to sit, the position is less solid than a down, and not nearly as comfortable for the dog. I happen to think that the down-stay is one of the most useful cues you can teach your dog. There are a million ways to use it.

So how do you teach the down-stay? Of course, your dog first needs to know how to do down. Most people who claim that their dog knows how to do it are only half-right; their dog can only do a down if they bend over at the waist and slap the ground a few times. Test your dog. Say "down" without bending over and see if she does anything other than stare at you. Now try the big bend and watch what happens. Dogs pick up on nonverbal cues more quickly than verbal ones, so you could essentially say "jelly doughnuts" and touch the ground and your dog will still assume the position. Your dog isn't listening to what you're saying—she's watching what your body is doing.

Let's clean that up, shall we? Start off by asking your dog to do a down the way you always have. If your dog didn't respond to the down test by actually doing the down when you said the word *down,* don't even bother saying the word. We'll add it later. If your dog requires that you have a treat in your hand in order to assume the position, give her a try without a treat in the pointer hand, but do clue her in that you have treats in your pocket. Give her the treat once she moves into position, and repeat the process a few times to get her into a down frame of mind.

A strong down-stay is one of the most helpful obedience cues.

The epicure

I often hear "My dog isn't motivated by treats," and to that I say, "Your dog isn't motivated by the treats *you're* using, but that doesn't mean she's not motivated by food!" I liken it to the difference between graham crackers and German chocolate cake. Both are desserts, but only one of the options makes *me* drool.

When I train, I use raw hot dogs cut into tiny, pinkie-fingernail-size pieces. I can't remember the last time a dog turned them down. Based on my observations, most dogs don't like dry bone-shaped treats. Opt for something moist, small, and stinky, like liver treats. **Remember:** Treats aren't supposed to be a meal replacement!

Here's where it starts to get tricky. Get her to do the down again, but this time instead of bending all the way over and touching the ground, let your pointer finger hover a few inches above the floor. She'll probably look at your strange new position and say, "I'm not sure what this means," but wait her out. Praise her quietly if you see anything that resembles the beginnings of a down, like a head-bob toward the ground or a foot shuffle that looks like she's getting ready to move into position. Yes, all the blood will rush to your head, but more than likely she'll realize that she just got rewarded for doing downs five times in a row, and this *kind of* looks like what you do when you want her to lie down, so she'll give it a shot. Major praise and a special treat when she figures it out!

Now you're home free. Bring your hand a little farther away from the ground on each successive attempt so that you're standing up straighter each time you ask her to assume the position. You're 90 percent there when you can stand completely straight and point to the ground, and your dog plops into position.

Now, what's missing? The word *down,* of course! You should add the word when you're able to get your dog to assume the position when you're standing up and subtly pointing to the ground. So stand up, point to the ground, and say "down" right as she slips into position. It'll take several repetitions before she makes the connection between your new body position, the word, and the behavior she's exhibiting. And there you have the back-saving down!

Time to move on to the meat of the behavior, the stay.

Ask your dog to do a down, and instead of giving her a treat, quietly praise her. (Don't forget to always praise your dog after she does the down but before she does the stay. This important step is often overlooked by my clients,

If your dog tries to tag your hand as she does the down, simply flip your wrist so that her nose can't connect with your hand.

so I usually stand a few steps away from their dog and say "gooood!" when she goes into the down.) Say "stay," and then take a baby step away to the left or right from where your dog is resting. (Don't take a step backward from your dog—that's the universal "Hey, follow me!" movement.) Return to your dog quickly, and give her a treat and lots of praise. Pretty simple, right?

If your dog was unable to hold the stay for a baby step, try it again but this time, instead of taking a full step away, keep one leg anchored right in front of her and lean your weight away on the opposite leg. It looks silly, but it works for those jumpy pups. Practice doing the stay taking baby steps in different directions, but don't be an overachiever—resist the urge to test your dog. Just because she can stay when you take two baby steps away doesn't mean that she's ready to hold a stay while you walk across the room with your back turned.

Dogs' bodies telegraph their intent, so keep an eye on your dog's body language as you practice the stay. Watch the back feet for telltale "I'm trying to get traction so that I can get up" behavior. If you notice your dog getting ready to get up, stand still, be quiet and wait for her to settle back down before you continue moving away from her.

Gradually add more steps away from your dog, always returning to her to give her a treat and praise. When your dog is comfortable with your moving ten steps away while facing her (don't trip on any furniture!), ask her to stay, turn your back, and take two steps away. This part can be difficult, because dogs always want to see our faces. Make it easy on your dog and only take a few steps with your back turned during your initial repetitions.

Once she feels comfortable when you walk across the room with your back turned to her, it's time to try leaving the room. Bring her close to a doorway, put her in a down-stay, and duck around the corner, keeping part of your body (maybe your foot or your elbow) visible. Make it quick and easy. Gradually ask her to hold a stay while you disappear completely around the corner and remain out of sight for a few seconds. Practice the behavior in different rooms throughout your house. When she's doing well with it, make it tougher by asking her to hold a stay in the middle of the room, cross the room with your back to her, disappear out of sight, and remain there for a short time. As always, come back and have a celebration.

Very superstitious

Many dogs tend to obsessively focus on the fingers and hand as they do the down. They touch, lick, or paw the fingers as they go into position. If your dog is kept from connecting with your fingers, she may seem unable to perform the behavior.

This is a "superstitious behavior," or something that she thinks is part of the desired behavior but actually isn't. Because you're taught to place a treat in your hand and let your dog sniff the treat as she goes into the down, your dog mistakenly assumes that the behavior you want goes like this, "I touch my nose to his fingers and sniff the treat in there, and then I put my belly on the ground, and then I get my treat."

The finger obsession isn't a problem until you start to transition your bending-over down to a standing-up down. Your dog still wants to tag your fingers—because that's part of the behavior—and she might try to jump up to reach your fingers before she does the down! I try to keep my canine students from falling into that trap by moving the treat from the pointer hand to a pocket after the first few successful repetitions, and not allowing them to tag my fingers as they move into position.

If your dog is having trouble stopping her finger habit because that's what she's been doing for ages, keep your hand in the same position but subtly flick your hand out of the way as she tries to tag it. This is one of those strange little behaviors that trips up many of my human clients!

The final step is the most difficult one: adding distractions. Distractions are anything you do that removes your attention from your dog or anything that presents a diversion for her. I've found that the majority of indoor distractions happen in the kitchen. Ask your dog to do a down-stay, and then walk over to the sink and turn on the water. Try opening the refrigerator. Wash a few dishes, sort the recycling—think of tasks that make sense in your household.

Outdoor distractions present a new set of challenges, so don't be surprised if your flawless indoor down-stay falls apart when you're outside. ***Remember:*** A stay in your backyard is something entirely different from a stay at the vet office or dog park. Just because your dog is a pro around the house doesn't mean that she'll be able to immediately assume the position in unfamiliar environments. Repeat to yourself, "It's not disobedience—she's still learning." It can take weeks to go from a simple down-stay in your family room to an outdoor distraction down-stay, so don't move faster than your dog can handle. If she's constantly breaking the stay, you've pulled a Tolstoy—go back to the last part of the equation where you and your dog were successful, and slowly rebuild from that step.

So you've put in your time and your dog now has a blisteringly beautiful down-stay—so what? What do you do with it? Break it out once a month as a party trick? Forget about it? Hardly. Down-stay is one of the most useful cues in the basic obedience repertoire. *How* you use it is dependent upon how well you've trained it. If you never got past the baby-steps-in-the-family-room stage, you can bet that your dog won't be able to hold a stay outdoors while a squirrel runs by. The saying "It works if you work it" applies to dog training as well.

Back to that blisteringly beautiful stay. Here are just a few ways you can use it around the house:

- Ask your dog to hold a down-stay while you prep her meals, and require that she hold it until you put her food down.

- Put your dog in a stay before you put her leash on instead of wrestling with her to get it on.

- Have your dog hold a stay while you're prepping your own dinner to keep her from getting underfoot.

- Use the stay to prevent your dog from racing out the door.

- Keep your dog from helping you load the dishwasher with a stay.

- Prevent your dog from following you into every room and up and down the stairs all day with a stay.

- Ask your dog to stay when you're at the counter paying for items at the pet store.
- Get your dog to stay when she steps on the scale at the vet's office.

I use the down-stay constantly with my guys, and, because of that, they assume the position without question. For some reason, Zeke refuses to move out of the way when people are walking near him—he just stands still and gets bulldozed. When I was cooking, Zeke's habit became dangerous. To avoid spilling a pot of boiling pasta, I taught Zeke and Sumner that they need to hang out in one specific area of the kitchen next to my prep counter. The moment they hear me begin chopping something, they both rush over to their special spot and assume a down-stay. They know as long as they're hanging out in that safe area, delicious goodies like tomatoes and cucumbers will rain down on them every so often. Zeke occasionally "forgets" that he's supposed to stay on the little carpet, and, when that happens, the consequence is that Sumner suddenly gets a jackpot of veggies and praise. Zeke quickly figures out that it's in his best interest to go back to the special spot. In my house, the down-stay isn't a party trick—it's a lifesaver!

Zeke and Sumner have figured out that it's a good idea to hold a down-stay when I make dinner.

Then what?

My clients will often ask me what to do if their dog acts "bad" and refuses to perform an obedience behavior. My first question is always "Does your dog truly know how to do the behavior?" (Confusion is often mistaken for insubordination.) If the answer is "yes," the conversation turns to consequences.

The person who is seamlessly weaving obedience training into his dog's daily life has a variety of consequences at his disposal when his dog opts to ignore an obedience cue. For example:

- If he asks his dog to sit before putting on the leash and the dog refuses, the consequence is that the leash gets dropped and the walk is momentarily called off.

- If his dog refuses to go to her bed while her dinner is prepped, the bowl is put back on the shelf and the vittle-fixin' process is halted.

- If the dog won't sit at a corner before crossing the street, the walk stops until she assumes the position.

- If the dog can't walk toward the dog park without pulling like a sled dog, forward motion toward the park stops.

Using treats during the training process might make you think that your dog is a slave to food and only food, but if you actually use the cues in her daily life, you'll see that you have a variety of payment options available to you. Your dog will soon learn that, treat or no treat, it's in her best interest to pay the piper.

Coming When Called

"My dog won't come when I call him." I hear that complaint far too often. I think one of the main reasons many dogs ignore the recall is because it usually means that the good times are over. Coming in from the yard, leaving the park . . . bah, who needs it? The other reason many dogs choose to ignore the recall is that punishment might not be far behind. "Fido! Get over here *now!*" you shout. Doesn't sound like much fun, does it?

I'll brag: most of my canine clients end up with a mighty impressive recall at the end of our lessons. I hear tales of former canine clients who slipped out the door to chase after the UPS guy, only to hear their person say the magic word and come tearing back inside. And then there was my shining recall duo, Claire and Oz the Briard. I was lucky enough to witness the strength of Oz's recall firsthand a few months after we completed training, and I'll never forget how blasé Claire was about it. I was floored by his responsiveness, but she acted as if it happened all the time. (It did.)

It was early morning and Claire and I were gathered with a group of eight other dog people in an unofficial city dog park. The dogs were frolicking pretty far away from their people, near the edge of the woods. Claire was gossiping, but I kept an eye on Oz. Suddenly, one of the other dogs spotted something deep in the woods—probably a rabbit—and he took off into the darkness after it. The rest of the dogs sped off after the lead dog.

"Claire, Claire, Oz is in the woods!" I yelled.

"Ozzie, *here!*" we shouted in unison. We clapped our hands and whistled, and a few moments later, out popped Oz. He galloped back to us, where we showered him with praise and special treats. The other dogs were nowhere to be seen, despite their owners' shouts for them. I was astounded by his response. Not only did he come back and ignore the hunt going on in the woods with his buddies, but he came back almost immediately! I kept my head bowed as I petted my appreciation to Oz so that Claire couldn't see the tears in my eyes. I was deeply touched by what I'd witnessed, and humbled that I'd had a part in building their amazing relationship. *This* is what a good bond looks like, I thought to myself.

On the flip side, you can practice the recall for ages but it won't be nearly as strong without a good bond. I worked with Lori and her Coton de Tulear, Gerti, prior to my dissection of what the bond is, and her results were yet another indication that, in relationship-challenged duos, training is not enough. Gerti was a major flight risk, which set off my bond alarm before I even knew it existed. Her family always had to slip out the door quickly lest Gerti dash out to play in traffic. When she did make it past them—and it happened frequently—it took them ages to corral Gerti and get her back home, so Lori called me for help. Gerti seemed slavishly devoted to me during our lessons, much like Daisy was (see chapter 1), which reinforced the idea that there was a bond issue afoot. We went through my standard course, and, while it was clear that Lori did her homework religiously, it wasn't having much of an impact on her relationship with Gerti. From what I saw during our lessons, it looked like fun was suspiciously absent from their relationship.

I ran into Lori at the grocery store a year later and asked whether Gerti was still running out the front door. She pursed her lips and nodded her head yes. "I can't understand it. We practiced the recall *all the time,* but she still wants to take off." Though I hadn't yet identified the specifics of the bond, I knew that their bond was in failure-to-thrive mode, and basic obedience training alone couldn't fix it.

The recall is probably the most public face of the bond you have, or don't have, with your dog. A recall-resistant dog is embarrassing because her lack of response shines a light on your relationship problems. Doesn't it feel like your dog just doesn't like you when she won't come when you call? All obedience training is entwined with the bond, but the recall is the heart and soul of the training/bond connection. Want to see what your relationship with your dog is made of? Work the recall, and you'll quickly find out.

When I teach the recall, I like to use a word other than *come* or the dog's name because by the time I show up on a client's doorstep, both of those words are usually the equivalent of verbal wallpaper; the dog has learned to ignore them. I like to reteach the recall using a brand-new word, *here,* which doesn't have any negative association. It's almost as if the recall with a different word is a totally different behavior from their previous exposure to coming when called. The goal is that your dog thinks that coming when called is incredibly fun, good things happen when she does it, and it doesn't always mean that the fun is ending. There are several rules that go along with reteaching the recall, and your adherence to them can make or break your success with it:

- **Rule #1: Use a happy tone of voice when you call your dog.** You don't have to sing the word *here* (though I get a huge kick out of it when big burly men do), but you should sound upbeat and happy when you say it. *Remember:* You want your dog to think the recall is a fun game.

- **Rule #2: Don't repeat the word *here*.** This is one of the more difficult rules because many of us seem to think that the moment the word has been uttered, our dogs should somehow magically teleport to our feet. It takes a few seconds for the sound to travel to your dog's ears, for her to digest what you said, and then for her to put the cue into action. Unless she's so far away that there's a question of whether she actually heard you, there's no need to repeat the word. Plus, if she gets used to hearing you say, "Here! Here! Here, girl, here!" she'll start to realize that you don't really mean it until you've said it half a dozen times. The goal is that you can say the word once, add some clapping or kissy noises if necessary, and your dog will come sailing to you.

- **Rule #3: Don't bribe.** You shouldn't have to show your dog that you have food or toys with you in order to get her to come to you. (If that's the case, she's holding her responses for ransom.) Saying "Hey, look what I have!" will only cause problems down the line when you *don't* have a goody with you. Granted, your dog should always get paid for responding to the recall while you're building the foundation behavior, but you shouldn't have to show her the goods before she performs the behavior.

- **Rule #4: Don't be an overachiever.** Building a strong recall takes time and patience. You'll need to incrementally build in new distractions, and practice in a variety of locations. *Remember:* Tolstoy, Tolstoy, Tolstoy. And don't forget the pond skating Olympian. . . . (see chapter 2).

With all that in mind, grab some tasty treats, it's time to start working on the recall!

It's best to start off working inside—we'll save the more difficult outdoor recalls for when Fido is more versed in the process. The first step is introducing the new recall word—*here*—and the fun it brings. Sit on the floor a few feet across from a friend or family member, and then say, "Here!" once, in a happy tone of voice. If your dog doesn't run to you right away (because you sound so darn happy, after all), clap your hands a few times, make kissy noises or whistling. As soon as she gets to you, give her a treat and have a party, making sure that she actually appreciates the type of party you're throwing. If she backs away from your petting, just use verbal praise and make sure to pay up with that treat. Have your partner call your dog next. After your dog figures out the running-back-and-forth game, which shouldn't take long, try hiding around corners or on different floors. You'll have to make more kissy and clapping noises at this stage of the recall, because she might not be able to detect exactly where you are in the house. The worst thing you can do is say "here" and just stand there in silence.

Check your dog's reactions to the game. Is she racing from person to person, or just lumbering along? (Granted, I've worked with a few Leonbergers for whom "lumber" was the only speed!) At this stage, the recall game should be super-easy and fun for her, and it should look like she's enjoying the process. If not, check yourself. How's your tone of voice? Are you having fun with it? Praising enough? You should also take a look at your body posture. Standing straight and glaring down at your dog can look a little scary to her during the early stages of the game (particularly if she has recall baggage). Try squatting down when you call her instead.

I do a strange but helpful recall exercise with my clients called the distraction recall as a precursor to doing outside recalls. The concept is simple: I tempt the dog with various intriguing items like an empty cat treat bag, a bit of real fox fur (don't ask), and old wool gloves that smell like treats, and the dog's owner has to do a recall so compelling that the dog ignores my distraction and runs to her owner. In a perfect world, I could hold out a steak in front of a dog's nose and she'd ignore it when her owner called "here!" (Haven't tried that one yet, but maybe someday!) The exercise is a stylized version of what happens when your dog discovers something beguiling in the hedgerow and you'd like her to come away from it. If you're consistent with your recall training, the word *here* almost elicits a reflexive response. You say the magic word and your dog is so conditioned to respond to it that she comes running. Be creative with your distractions. Hairbrushes, dirty socks, and bottles of lotion are all reliable canine temptations. Ask your helper to hold the item so that your dog can smell it but not actually interact with it, and then call "here!" and hope for the best. (You'll probably have to throw in some extra kissy noises!) Praise your dog if she stops sniffing the item and looks at you when she hears you call. She's trying to make a choice between you and the distraction, and you want her to make the right one! As always, give her a tasty treat and big praise when she gets to you.

If your dog is responding quickly and joyfully to every "here!" after a few weeks of practice in your house, you can try recalls in your backyard. Switch to a new, high-value treat when you move from indoors to outdoors, because you're now competing with distractions much more interesting than the contents of your home. If you've been using hot dogs, try cheese. Apartment dwellers without yards can practice recalls in the hallway during off-hours. The city dogs I work with seem to love racing down the hall—plus, it's good practice for if your dog ever slips out your front door. If hallway recalls aren't an option, look for a neighborhood fenced tennis court with flexible pet rules (or if you're like me, pretend you didn't see the NO PETS ALLOWED sign!). You and your helper should stand about twelve feet apart when you start working on outdoor recalls, and then as your dog gets more confident with the exercise, move farther apart. If you have a wooded lot, hide behind trees and have her try to find you when you say "here." To keep it fun, move to a new spot each time she discovers your hiding spot.

One of my favorite outside recall exercises is the runaway recall. Call your dog and then turn and run away as she starts heading toward you. Slow down as she catches up to you and give her a big reward. (Try whipping out a toy when she gets to you and playing a quick round of tug.) This game taps into a dog's innate desire to chase, so even the slowest dogs might decide to kick it into overdrive when they see you running away!

Teaching the recall is actually a simple, straightforward process—it just takes time and creativity. It's important to use some sort of tangible reward—high-value treats or toys—for several months during the training process and beyond. Your dog doesn't *have* to come to you when she's off-leash running around in your backyard, so make it worth her while to listen to you when you call. Pay her for a job well done!

Go to Bed

I can't say enough good things about the cue "go to bed." I love to teach it, I love to watch dogs doing it, and I love figuring out new ways to apply it. I've been suggesting different dog supplies throughout this book, but I think you should put a fabulous new dog bed at the top of your shopping list. Of course, many dogs don't need their own beds because they get couch privileges, but for those households that don't allow dogs on furniture, like mine, get a bed. In fact, get a few beds. I've found that most dogs prefer to have a bolster-style bed or doughnut bed, one that has an edge they can lean against. Those ubiquitous flat, round, plaid, hunting-catalog beds might look good in the pictures, but my experience has shown that dogs don't love them as much as the beds with bolsters.

Most dogs prefer a bed that has a bolster that they can lean against.

Because Zeke and Sumner aren't allowed on the furniture in our house (the farting, snoring, and dirty paws are prohibitive), I have dog beds in almost every room for them. Their home-base bed is in the family room next to the couch; plus, we have one in the kitchen, one in my office, and two in the workroom. (They actually prefer to share a bed even though it looks cramped and uncomfortable!) No matter what room we're in, I can guarantee that they're hanging out on their bed, even during the heat of summer. We always take a bed when they travel with us so that they have consistency, even in an unfamiliar environment.

Teaching your dog to go to bed when asked is an incredibly useful behavior that doubles as an impressive party trick. Nothing says "Check out how clever my dogs is!" like sending her to her bed from another room. (Perhaps that's why placement cues like "go to bed" are often overlooked—the behavior seems too cool to be useful!) An additional bonus of teaching your dog this behavior is that it hones your skills as a trainer. The exercise requires great powers of observation during the initial stages. You'll learn to really watch your dog, and you'll see the "light-bulb moment" when your dog seems to say, "Ohhhh, I get it now!" Another major bonus? Working on "go to bed" will exhaust your dog!

My former client Maxie was an irrepressible, apartment-dwelling Boston Terrier. Her owners, Jeff and Liz, knew that she was clever—too clever, in fact—and they couldn't figure out how to direct her boundless energy. Walks around the city took the edge off, but she was often restless and prone to sock thievery. (She was a collector, not a destroyer, mind you.) I'm partial to Bostons, of course, so I was eager to get to work with the mischievous little clown.

She aced her basic obedience lessons but seemed to trip up when it came time to do bed work at the second lesson. She'd go into a sit and a down, and then she'd jump on me as if to say, "What, lady? What do you want me to do?!" It seemed that our little genius was hitting a wall, but we knew that Maxie had it in her. Liz vowed to give bed training her full attention in between our lessons.

Sure enough, Liz had a surprise for me the following week. "Watch this," she said with a smile. "Maxie, bed!" Maxie tore out of the family room and into the kitchen where her bed was kept. She hopped on it and collapsed into a down, smiling the whole time.

"That's huge!" I hollered, which made Maxie come running back into the family room to share in the excitement. "She's already acing stuff that I wasn't planning on teaching for a few weeks! How did you do it?"

"I just kept at it," Liz replied, reaching down to give Maxie a pat. "The first few attempts were really rough. Maxie seemed frustrated because she couldn't figure out what I wanted her to do. She knew it had something to do with the bed, but she kept doing sits and downs right next to it and sort of avoided getting on it. Then, about two days into training, it was like she just *got* it. She deliberately took her paw, placed it on the bed and looked right at me. I shrieked so loudly I think I scared her! That was the light-bulb moment you were talking about, right?"

"Exactly. Cool, huh?"

"*So* cool! From that point on she was unstoppable. It was like she was reading my mind. She loves working on bed, so we spent a ton of time on it. And the best part was that it really wore her out. I'd work on it after our evening walk, when she normally bounces off the walls and keeps me from watching TV. I swear, ten minutes of bed practice and she was done for the night!"

I gave Liz some much-deserved praise, and we got ready to begin our lesson.

"Where's Maxie?" I asked.

We looked around and spotted her on her bed a room away, leaning to the side so that she could see us through the doorway. Our little student had grown bored with all the talking and opted to settle herself into a position that she knew would earn her some recognition! Teaching go to bed can initially be challenging for some dogs, as it was for Maxie. Unlike sit or down, it's not something dogs do naturally. Plus it's a multistep process—first your dog has to learn to walk toward the bed, then get on it, then settle comfortably, and then hang out on the bed for a bit.

Go to bed is one exercise where the clicker streamlines the process. I've taught the behavior using a marker word like *yup,* but I've found that dogs that are trained with a clicker understand the process more quickly. Some of the movements you're looking for are fleeting, which is why the precision of the clicker is so helpful. The exercise is essentially a stylized version of the old childhood game hot-or-cold. The clicker is used to tell your dog "You're getting warmer, you're getting warmer" as she tries to figure out why the bed is sitting in the middle of the kitchen floor. (It helps to bring the bed to a room that doesn't have carpet. The difference between the floor texture and the bed texture makes the game a little easier for dogs.)

The process starts as soon as you throw the bed onto the floor. Your dog will probably sniff it or look over at it. Click and treat her—game on! From this point, click and treat anything that looks like your dog showing an interest in the bed. She might look at the bed again or take a step toward it. Click! If she's having trouble getting started, you can click even if she flicks her eyes toward the bed. ***Remember:*** This is the hot-and-cold game, so anything that looks like the beginning of interest in the bed is click-worthy.

If she keeps putting her paw on the bed but nothing else, withhold the click for one repetition and see whether she offers you a more pronounced version of the behavior. She might tap her paw on the bed again, and then once more, and then, because you haven't click-treated her in a few repetitions, she might offer a bigger, more obvious version of the behavior, like putting *both* feet on the bed, just to make sure that you see it. You get what you click, so if you keep click-treating the same behavior over and over again, that's all she's ever going to give you!

Once she's getting at least partway on the bed, make sure to give her a reward so that she's on the bed when she receives it. So if she's putting her two front feet on the bed, click and give her the treat while she's still on the bed—don't move her off the bed to give her the treat. In the beginning, it helps to give the reward exactly where the behavior should be happening. You want your dog to end up on the bed, so reward her on the bed. She'll probably figure out that, since she's already performed the behavior that got her the click-treat, she'll have to figure out something *else* to do in order to get the treat. She might move forward on the bed. Click-treat. She might move so far forward that her back feet go onto the bed. *Major* click-treat! Once all four feet are on the bed, she might collapse into a down. We have a winner, click-treat!

Teaching go to bed is a helpful household cue, and an impressive trick!

Your dog should soon figure out that she needs to get all the way on the bed in order to get paid. Once that happens, you can begin adding a name for her new skill. I like to use the word *bed,* but I've heard everything from *home* to *night-night* used for this behavior. Again, your dog won't know what the word *bed* means, so you need to teach her English. Softly say "bed" right as she crosses the threshold. I said "softly" because if you shout "bed!" she'll probably stop dead in her tracks and think, "What?" It'll take about twenty repetitions before she makes the connection between what you're saying and what she's doing. When you get through the behavior naming process, you'll be able to say the word *bed* and your dog should get right on.

At this point, she's probably figuring out that being on the bed is a very good thing. She might get on, collapse into a down, and decide that she's not going to get off. Why interrupt a good thing? This is where the treats happen, after all. The best thing to do in this scenario is click her for getting on the bed, and then toss the treat so that it lands a few steps away from the bed and she has to get off to get it. It's like hitting the reset button. She gets off the bed to collect her treat, which gives you a chance to start the process over again.

After she's getting on the bed reliably when you stand next to it, it's time to lessen her dependence on your proximity to the bed. (It sometimes seems like she's getting on the bed only because you're standing right in front of it!) Click-treat her for getting on the bed, toss the treat off the bed so that she has to get up to get it, and then take a baby step away from the bed while she's retrieving the treat. If she's in a rhythm, she'll probably get right back on the bed, not noticing that you're no longer standing right next to it. Click-treat her again, toss the treat, and take another step away. Repeat the process, taking a small step away each time she gets off the bed to retrieve her treat. Before you know it, you'll be halfway across the room from the bed!

Your dog may get conflicted when you've moved more than three steps away from the bed. She sees you standing far away from it and wonders how in the world she's ever going to get paid, because treat dispensing always happens right at your feet. This new wrinkle presents her with a dilemma. You can solve the crisis by clicking when she gets on the bed and then tossing the treat to her on the bed from where you're standing. It helps to have a good pitching arm so that the treat ends up right in front of her feet!

You've now achieved your foundation bed behavior. Time to move on to the tough stuff. The next time she gets on the bed, wait a few seconds before you click. This helps to teach her that going to bed can be a long-term behavior, not a drive-by trick. Continue padding in more duration, a few seconds at a time, before you click-treat each time she goes to her bed, occasionally throwing in a quick one now and then.

Confused about whether you should toss the treat to her while she's on the bed or toss it to make her get off the bed? From this point on, toss the treat *off* the bed if you want to reset the behavior and start over. Toss the treat to her while she's still *on* the bed if you're trying to prolong the amount of time she stays on it. You can transition off the clicker when she's reliably responding to the word *bed,* and use a release like "all done" or "free" when you're ready for her to get off the bed. Training a release is simple; say "all done" in a happy tone of voice and bend over slightly so that she understands that she can get off the bed.

The final step is adding distractions to the behavior. Real life looks very different from training time, which means you're not as keenly focused on your dog when you're trying to make breakfast or unpack groceries as you are during training time. Unfortunately, many dogs seem to think, "Huh, we must be done working now because he's not staring at me anymore," and then get up and go about their business. Help your dog understand that even if you're not looking directly at her, if you ask her to go to bed and hang out, she should do just that until you tell her, "All done!" You can begin to drive that point home by engaging in small tasks after you've sent her to bed, like washing a few dishes or sorting through your mail. Toss her treats while she rests on the bed so that she understands that she'll continue to get paid if she rests quietly there.

If you practice, the finished product could look like this: You tell your dog "bed" from across the room and she runs over, gets on, and lays down on it. You praise. She calmly remains there, occasionally getting a treat from you for hanging out so patiently, until you tell her "All done!" The hope is that the positive training associations will encourage her to seek out the bed even if you're not actively training.

So how can you put go to bed to work in your everyday life?

- Send your dog to bed when you're trying to unpack groceries or load the dishwasher.
- Ask her to hang out on her bed while you eat dinner instead of begging next to the table.
- Bring a bed with you when you travel and encourage her to relax on it so that she doesn't become overwhelmed by her new surroundings.
- Use the bed to help her transition from sleeping in your bed or on the couch.
- Keep the bed handy when you have guests visiting so that your dog can have a "home base" away from the activity hub.
- Send her to the bed in your office when you want to work on the computer undisturbed.

If you're really, really motivated to train, teach her that she should go to her bed when she hears the doorbell and remain there as you welcome your guests or pay for the pizza. (I've only had one client achieve this behavior with his dog and it was *amazing*. The bed was two rooms away from the front door!)

Leash Walking

Ah, leash walking. The most challenging, frustrating, potentially annoying behavior in the basic obedience handbook. Although it takes patience and attentiveness to train polite leash walking, it's not a mentally taxing assignment for walker or walkee. You'll soon see that the polite leash walking concepts are straightforward.

The challenge is that it isn't easy to untrain a committed puller. The simple fact is that dogs do it because it works. They pull, we follow. Pulling typically takes root in puppyhood, much like jumping up. A small puppy eager to move forward fast seems harmless, so the behavior is left unchecked until that same cute little puppy starts piling on the pounds and hitting her adult weight. Before you know it, you're dealing with a straining behemoth who pulls with a force that leaves your arm numb after every walk.

The recall is probably the most obvious display of your bond with your dog, but polite leash walking is a close second. When I see a dog pulling at the very end of her leash, I see an obedience problem coupled with a bond issue. Why isn't that dog motivated to walk closer to her owner? And why doesn't the person care that his dog is walking twelve feet away from him?

One of my neighbors walks her small black dog on an extendible leash. She's usually chatting on her cellphone as she passes my house (which is a few streets over from hers, so that means that she's probably been chatting for a while), and her dog is at the end of the leash pulling as hard as she can. I'm amazed at the disconnect between them. Each one is busy with an individual task, separated only by a leash but looking as if there are miles between them. Based on the way they look during their walks, my neighbor probably considers leash time a chore to endure rather than a chance to strengthen her relationship with her dog.

Leash walks are yet another opportunity to grow the bond with your dog, and the only way to really do that is through cooperative, proximity-based walking. When you walk your dog, you should be experiencing the world together, enjoying the scenery, and acting as a team to take on whatever comes around the next corner.

It will come as no surprise to learn that I'm particular about leash-walking equipment. I'm not flexible about leashes—I don't like those leashes that extend upwards of fifteen feet from a plastic handle. In fact, I despise them. Many of my clients bring them out when it's time to work on leash walking, and I launch into the Gospel of the Six-Foot Leash, or, Why Flexible Leashes Are the Devil. Flexible leashes might seem like a fantastic concept: They give your dog room to roam! They allow her to run back and forth and wear herself out while you stroll along! But they can actually be dangerous. How so? Most dogs walked on retractable leashes spend their time at the very end of it. Because of the leash length, the dog is exposed to whatever comes around the corner long before her owner is. Before you know it, your dog is face-to-face with the aggressive dog from down the street, and the other dog has already initiated a rumble before you've had a chance to react. Or on the flip side, if *your* dog is the neighborhood menace, she's tangoing with the sweet puppy or baby in a stroller or squirrel crossing the road before you can even think to reel her in. Then there's that locking mechanism on the handle. Owners flex their fly-fishing muscles when they do the lock-pull-lock-pull maneuver to try to reel their dogs in closer when trouble is afoot. Imagine the potential disaster that can occur if you're unable to slap the lock down fast enough or if the lock fails. I once heard the sad story of a city dog on a flexible leash who rounded a corner faster than her person, darted out into the street, and was hit by a car.

Take another look at that thin cord that connects the flexible walker to the flexible walkee. Combine a motivated puller with a brazen bunny and the walker is left with a useless piece of plastic in his hand while his dog disappears over the horizon. I'm not suggesting that you need a three-inch-thick leash to keep your dog safe, but I do think that the security provided by the thin cord on a retractable leash is questionable at best.

Thick or thin?

Though I think the thin cord on flexible leashes is unsafe, thicker is not necessarily better when it comes to leashes. I've seen far too many puppies wearing massive Cujo-sized leashes and saddled with the heavy clasp that comes with them.

Leashes that thick are uncomfortable and unnecessary. I keep a ¾-inch leather leash in my bag (for those households that still need to be talked out of using flexible leashes), and I'll use that same thin leash on every dog from a 10-week-old Lab puppy to an adult Giant Schnauzer. Bonded leash walking negates the need for a titanium-strength leash, because a bonded leash walker isn't straining at the end of it. A thin leather leash is just enough to keep your dog close and safe. Plus, it's more comfortable for both of you!

There's a hidden obedience component to flexible leashes as well. Dogs have *opposition reflex,* which means that when they feel tension pulling on their necks, their reflex is to pull forward. Because the flexible leash is always tense to keep the dog from tripping over the excess cord, the dog gets used to the feeling of tension around her neck and comes to understand that a tight leash equals forward movement. Unfortunately, the core concept of polite leash walking is that a tight leash means that the walk *stops,* and a loose leash means that the walk can continue. If the owner decides to transition off the flexible leash, the dog has to relearn the loose-leash concept.

I adore six-foot leather leashes as much as I abhor flexible leashes. I prefer a soft, unvarnished leather that becomes more pliant with age. They're comfortable to hold and they're incredibly strong. Six feet of freedom is just enough room to allow for exploration and elimination, but not so much that your dog's safety is at risk. Plus it allows you to participate in the walk as a team. Sumner is a very nervous leash walker, but he's much more confident when he's close to me. When he gets frightened by a barking dog or a rumbling garbage truck, I'm right by his side to work him through his fear. Imagine the how difficult that would be if Sumner were on a flexible leash walking fifteen feet in front of me.

The good news about leash training is that the core concepts are straightforward and easy to digest. The bad news is that you actually need to focus on what you're doing when you walk your dog. That means you'll need to hang up the cellphone, stop looking in your neighbors' windows, and pay attention to your dog. The other bit of bad news is that there's no such thing as training walks and regular walks. Every time you're outside walking your dog, she's learning. Permitting impolite behavior on some walks and disallowing it during others will create training inconsistency and prolong the process—and probably confuse the heck out of your dog!

I like to use a thin leather leash for walks. It's more comfortable to hold than a thick cotton leash. Plus, it's lighter and more comfortable for your dog to wear.

Though I've done leash training without the clicker with many dogs (including Sumner, because the sound used to scare him), I prefer to use a clicker whenever possible. Much like bed training, there are numerous fleeting teachable moments that occur during leash training that can be clicked and strengthened. The clicker also helps to cut through environmental clutter present during every leash walk. Your voice might be muffled by traffic and construction noises, but the sound of the clicker can cut right through it. If you opt to do leash training without a clicker, make sure that you've conditioned your marker word prior to using it outside and that your dog knows to look at you to collect her treat when she hears the word.

Before we get started with the logistics of leash walking, let's talk about leash juggling. Although the core leash-walking concept is easy (pulling = stop, slack = go), you *will* go through an awkward learning-the-dance phase as you get started. You're going to be dealing with two hands' worth of equipment (and that's not counting a full poop bag!), so the mechanics of where you hold what matter. Each hand has an important job during the walk. One hand is used to hold the leash and clicker, while the other hand is dedicated to treat delivery. The hand you use to click is largely dependent on whether you're a righty or a lefty, and will determine what side of your body your dog walks on. If you click with your

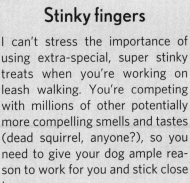

Stinky fingers

I can't stress the importance of using extra-special, super stinky treats when you're working on leash walking. You're competing with millions of other potentially more compelling smells and tastes (dead squirrel, anyone?), so you need to give your dog ample reason to work for you and stick close to you.

right hand, it's easier to use your left hand to deliver treats to your dog who is walking on your left and vice versa. If you try to use your right hand to deliver treats to your dog who is walking on your left, she'll be forced to cross in front of your feet and will end up tripping you. Likewise, keeping your leash and treats in the same hand, or the clicker and treats in the same hand will force you to do a juggling act every time you try to reward your dog. (You might accidentally offer your dog the clicker instead of the treat, or you might lose precious time dropping the clicker to dig through your pocket to find a treat.) Keeping one hand dedicated to treats will also cut down the excess saliva and grease on the rest of your paraphernalia!

I'll hammer the point home once more: a tight leash means "stop" and a loose leash means "go." Relearning is usually required on both ends of the leash, as many people don't even recognize when the leash is tight or only consider it tight when the dog is at a full-tilt pull. My definition of a "stop" leash is when the leash is completely straight and there's no curve in it between you and your dog.

Leash walking can be a juggling act when clicker training. Try keeping your leash and clicker in the same hand, leaving your other hand free to carry just the treats.

Once you've got the leash, clicker, and treat mechanics figured out, it's time to hit the road. Begin walking with your dog on whichever side feels more comfortable for you, but make sure that you actually like where she's walking, because you'll need to be consistent. Click-treat if she manages to take a step or two next to you before she dashes off. This immediately tells her that she'll get a greasy paycheck for hanging out next to you. Some of the most dedicated pullers I've worked with have had their light-bulb moment after just a few initial click-treats during their first walks. They quickly decide that hanging out close to their owners and getting paid is a very good thing indeed, and they morph into reformed pullers almost immediately. I love it when that happens! From that point on, it's just a matter of varying how often your dog gets click-treated.

It doesn't always happen that way, though. Suppose you walked out your door loaded up with your clicker, goodies, and a positive attitude, only to have your dog speed past you the moment you opened the door and never look back. Welcome to how the rest of the world starts off with leash training. The *second* the leash goes straight, stop walking. One of two things will happen: Either your dog will continue pulling as if you're just an anchor she's trying to lose, or she'll glance back at you with a look that says, "Huh?

Why'd we stop?" If your dog goes the "Huh?" route, click her for her attention (it's actually a big deal that she looked back at you), and encourage her to come back to your side in order to collect the treat instead of reaching out to her to give her the treat. You want her to understand that treats happen in the "hot zone" next to your leg. Eventually, she'll figure out that walking in that spot is a good idea because that's where the treats happen.

It's highly likely that your dog will collect her treat and rush off to the end of the leash again. Never fear—all is not lost. Simply stop walking again and look for that glance back at you. Repeat the click-treating sequence, but this time try to slip in another click-treat before she dashes off to the end of the leash again. Take a few steps. Is she staying next to you? Click-treat, making sure to reward her in the hot zone next to your leg instead of reaching out to give her the treat. The hot-zone aspect trips many people up, but it's important to pay her in that area because that's where you want her to end up when you walk—plus, it helps keep your dog from zigzagging back and forth in front of you or circling behind you.

Your dog doesn't have to walk directly next to you in order to earn a click-treat during this early phase of the process. *Anything* other than pulling can be rewarded. In fact, the more you click in the beginning, the less you'll have to click in the long run. Frequent click-treating leaves little doubt in your dog's mind about what "works" on a leash walk.

If she dashed to the end of her leash and didn't look back at you when you stopped, you're going to have to do a penalty yard. A *penalty yard* is a dog-safe punishment that requires you to slowly move backward (don't turn around and retreat—just walk backward, and don't jerk or pull at your dog), losing ground until your dog realizes that she's covering old real estate and gives you the "huh?" look. Again, click-treat when you get the look, and require her to come back to your side to collect the treat; then keep moving forward.

The key to a well-executed penalty yard is to keep backing up until your dog gives you that look over her shoulder. If you abandon the process before you get any sort of acknowledgment from your dog, the retreat won't really have any meaning. Requiring that look is a way of telling your dog, "I'm here on this walk with you."

Click-treat *anything* that isn't a full-tilt pull, and click-treat *anything* that resembles polite leash walking, even if it doesn't look perfect. If she's walking three steps ahead of you, but the leash still has a curve in it, click-treat,

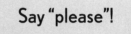

Say "please"!

It's always a good idea to ask your dog to sit before you open the front door to go for a walk. It's safer than having her pull you out the door—plus, it reinforces the "you scratch my back, I'll scratch yours" aspect of the bond. You'll gladly open the door for her if she sits for you first.

making sure to pay her in the hot zone next to your leg. If she veers off to sniff something in a yard, click-treat her as she's heading back toward you. (Though I encourage close walking, I'm not a leash-walking dictator. Let her stop and read the pee-mail. Let her roll in the grass. Leash walks should allow your dog to check out the neighborhood and leave her mark.) If she happens to look up at you during the walk, click-treat her and then get on your knees and thank the training gods, because you've just experienced a miracle! Looking up at you during a walk is one-third of the polite leash-walking holy trinity. (The other two-thirds are a loose leash and keeping similar pacing.) It's a sign that she's figuring out that there are two bodies attached to the leash and that it makes sense to check in with you during the walk.

When your dog is pulling *toward* something like a dried earthworm on the sidewalk, instead of just pulling because that's how walks usually go, you'll have to repeat the penalty yard a few times in a row before she realizes that her pulling is actually making her move farther away from her goal. There's a double reward aspect in goal-oriented pulling. Not only does she earn a click-treat for walking politely next to you and not surging toward the goal, but once she figures out that pulling isn't working and sticks close to you, she'll get to check out the distraction.

This is an example of a fine leash walk: There's a gentle curve in the leash, and the dog and person are walking at a similar pace.

"This way!"

I love the casual leash-walking cue, "This way!" It's a friendly alert that lets your dog know that you're going to walk in a different direction, which keeps her from getting jerked off her feet if she's too busy sniffing something to notice that you've decided to change direction. It's a teach-as-you-go kind of cue: I've found that even brand-new canine clients instinctively follow when I cheerfully call out, "This way!" To teach it, say the phrase just as you're beginning to change direction, and add some kissy noises if necessary. It's simple to teach, and it's helpful to have it in the training repertoire!

If your dog fights the penalty yard and makes you look like you're torturing her as you back up, or if she opts for civil disobedience and sits down and refuses to budge, try the slackening technique: When she pulls, stop walking and then slowly release the tension on the leash by moving your arm toward your dog. If she takes the newfound slack and tries to dash off again, stop moving, wait a moment, and then try to offer her some slack again. If she remains still as you slacken the leash and doesn't try to pull ahead, begin walking and click-treat if she manages to go a few steps without pulling.

I can't stress how important generosity is during the early stages of leash training. Stingy clicking is the number-one reason why people have a hard time with the process. If your dog only gets one click-treat every two blocks, I can guarantee that you're missing out on a bunch of fantastic little teachable moments in between those blocks. Every click-treat is providing your dog with important information about what you like, what works, and what keeps the walk moving forward. You're not looking for perfection in the early training stages—just an understanding that pulling = stop and slack = go + treats.

I keep referring to the "early stages of the process." So what happens once your dog is earning plenty of click-treats for her behavior, she's keeping her pace similar to yours and pulling less? Then it's time to refine. You're going to make her work harder to earn her click-treats. Instead of clicking her for walking three steps ahead of you with a slack leash, wait for her to slow down so that she's walking right next to you before you click. Instead of clicking her every few steps, make her walk for a longer period of time in between clicks. Wait for her to glance up at you before you click.

This is the beginning of the weaning process so that you don't have to spend the rest of your life with a pocket full of treats. If you've been consistent with training, she knows that she's probably going to get paid at some point—she's just not sure when. Much like a gambler will sit at a slot machine for hours waiting for a $10 payout, your dog will walk next to you waiting for her next jackpot.

Loose leash walking should become second nature for her. Instead of pulling madly, she'll discover that life is much more pleasant when she stays close to you and she'll choose to hang out there. That's actually the reason I don't teach the word *heel*. You shouldn't have to *tell* your dog to walk close to you—she'll just choose to do it naturally because that's how walks work!

It's unfortunate, but leash pulling has a fairly high relapse rate after training. That point was driven home for me when I accidentally busted my former client Denise for letting her dog, Brandy, drag her down the street. I happened to be in her neighborhood working on leash walking with a new client, and we ran into them during a walk. I could tell Denise didn't recognize me as we were approaching from a few blocks away, which gave me an opportunity to watch the spectacle of Denise trying to keep up with her exuberant Irish Setter. Once we got closer and she realized it was I, she slammed on the brakes and smiled guiltily.

"You caught me," she said, as Brandy strained like a bronco at the end of the leash. Brandy's pulling was compounded by the fact that she, too, realized that the Treat Lady was a mere ten feet away.

"Wow, Denise, what happened?" I asked. "Brandy was a really awesome leash walker last summer. Where did we go wrong?"

"Life just got in the way, I guess. The girls went back to school, so my schedule got busier, and I had to do shorter walks. When I had a free moment to walk Brandy, I just wanted her to get out and get some exercise, so I guess I slacked off on the rules."

A tight leash like this one means that the walk should stop.

"Well, it's never too late to start over," I said, trying to sound upbeat even though I was disappointed at how things had turned out for Denise and Brandy.

I always tell my clients that leash walking is a "marathon" behavior. Polite leash walking requires a slow and steady approach, particularly for dogs who have been pulling for a while. The initial "fix" can happen quickly, but making it stick requires dedication and, more important, patience. I'll be the first to admit that polite leash walking is tough. I realize that it's easier just to tune out during a leash walk and let your dog pull. I understand that doing penalty yards in front of your neighbor's house is embarrassing. If you're serious about reforming your puller, you just have to stick with it. As they say in rehab, it works if you work it.

Chapter 6

BUILDING BLOCK #2: BE PREDICTABLE BUT UNPREDICTABLE

Dogs are excellent timekeepers. My dogs, Zeke and Sumner, are so reliable about telling me when it's dinnertime that I don't even have to look at the clock. They know when it's Sunday, and they expect a walk as soon as our leisurely breakfast is finished. Many of the dogs I work with know when I'm due to arrive on the front step, and they dutifully wait near the door for me. Dogs have an uncanny knack for understanding household rhythms, and that includes almost Swiss-watch timekeeping. That gift—or curse, depending on how you look at it—can work in your favor if you temper your dog's need for predictability with some surprising inconsistency each day.

The idea behind daily unpredictability is that you, the Keeper and Controller of All Good Things, can at any moment decide to do something amazingly fun and creative. Your dog never knows what you're going to do next! Sometimes you make a special treat or toy appear out of your pocket. You might occasionally stop working at your computer and play a round of tug. You've been known to shut off the TV during the news and do some trick training. You invite him along when you're going to your bank's drive-through window. You're unpredictable (in a good way, of course).

The only things that are consistent in Zeke and Sumner's lives are meal times, potty times, and sleep times. Other than those touchstones, life is one surprise after another. One of my favorite ways of making life unpredictable for them is taking them for a walk when they don't expect one. There was a period when I was boring and stuck to a predictable walk schedule, between two o'clock and three o'clock every day. Their timekeeping skills made my life miserable from 1:30 on ("Is it time yet? Can we go? Are you ready now?"), so I decided to shake up their lives and take walks whenever the mood struck or my workload lightened. I had to fight through some canine backlash in the beginning of the transition, when they became convinced that my clock must be broken. ("Hey, you over there. It's walk time. Yoo-hoo! Remember us and that walking thing we do every day? Yeah, it's time.")

Hmmm...

Most dogs recognize the word *walk*, but I decided to be different and teach my dogs that when I look at them, pause, and say, "Hmmm... I have a *really* good idea," it means that we're going to take a walk. On some days I'll just say "Hmmm," and on others I'll abruptly stop working at my computer and say, "I have a *really* good idea." That's enough to kick off their happy dance. I do have to be careful, though, because I've caught them looking at me with excitement when they hear me say "Hmmm" in conversation!

Now, some days we walk at seven o'clock in the morning; other days it's three o'clock in the afternoon. One of the benefits: because we no longer have a set time, they aren't able to pester me when they think they're "due" a walk. Granted, I get lots of sad looks if five o'clock rolls around and we haven't seen pavement yet, but they know that the chance exists that I'll get a nutty idea at 5:30 and suggest a walk. I love the looks on their faces when I choose an unusual time. They're used to napping from eight o'clock until ten o'clock on most days, so when I change things up and interrupt their nap for a walk, they give me the most adorable, incredulous looks! "Really?" They seem to say, "*Now?*"

Adding unpredictability to your dog's life will keep him guessing about what comes next. Though I've said that dogs thrive on a schedule, the unpredictability I'm suggesting will not negatively impact the scheduling your dog requires to be happy and healthy. Adding unpredictability to your dog's life doesn't mean making him eat lunch instead of dinner, or denying him a walk one day and then giving him two walks on the next day. Little shifts in your dog's daily routine will shake things up enough so that he wants to look to you to figure out what adventures come next. You're no longer the dull two-squares-and-a-walk-around-the-block person he's used to. Instead, you're a bundle of little Christmas morning surprises every day. You want him to look at you and think, "I need to pay attention to this person because I never know what she's going to do next!" The good news is that adding unpredictability to your dog's life is easier than you might imagine. It doesn't cost a penny, and it'll grow your bond like a weed!

Walk around the Clock

I've already suggested that changing up your walk schedule is a good idea, but I realize that not everyone has the luxury of offering their dog a midday stroll. You might have only a 20-minute window in the morning and an hour or so in the evening to get the job done. That was the case with my client

Ryan and his chocolate Lab rescue named Cooper. Ryan was looking to fast-track his bond with Cooper because they were setting off on a cross-country road trip in the fall. They were off to an excellent start with their basic obedience training, but Ryan wanted to do everything possible to cement his relationship with Cooper before they hit the road. He wanted Cooper to be a well-mannered, responsive dog during their trip, so we brainstormed about bonding options.

Because Ryan had an office job (that he was about to ditch in favor of the open road), he couldn't offer Cooper a flexible walking schedule. I asked Ryan to break down his daily walk routine for me.

"Well, I give him a quickie in the morning before I leave for work, and then my roommate comes home for lunch and lets him out in the backyard. I get home at 5:30, and then we go for a 45-minute walk before it gets dark."

"Okay, not bad. Tell me about your walk route."

"Well, I basically do two versions of the same walk route. In the morning, we head down toward the park and then circle back after about ten minutes, and then in the evening we keep going all the way down to the park and then come back. It's a decent walk."

"Sure, it sounds pretty good. But I have an idea for you: Change your route up every day. Pick a new direction instead of walking the same road every day. The walks you're giving him are decent from an exercise perspective, but they're boring! He's habituating to everything he encounters on the walk, so the first time you make a pit stop during your road trip he's going to have his mind blown by the newness of everything. Let's try a new walk route today and see how it goes."

Instead of taking the same route we'd done on the two prior lessons, we took the road less traveled. Up until that point we'd been lulled by Cooper's laid-back approach to our walks on the everyday route. Ryan was amazed to discover how much Cooper changed once he was on the unfamiliar terrain. Cooper walked much faster on the new route. He didn't pull, but there was a bounce to his step that was missing when we walked on the familiar terrain. He was more interested in his surroundings. He urinated more frequently. Cooper seemed to enjoy the change in venue, and Ryan enjoyed the change in his dog.

"See the difference? We're only one street over from your usual walk but Cooper is acting like we're in a different state!"

Ryan continued to change his walk routes with Cooper, and though he couldn't change the time of day that they walked, he added more unpredictability by altering the duration of the walk. He occasionally woke up a few minutes earlier so that he could take a longer walk with Cooper in the morning, or tacked on an extra loop in the evening. Cooper's once predictable outdoor life became a fun guessing game. Each day, the destination was unknown, which gave him a taste of what he was about to experience with Ryan once they hit the road.

Taking the road less traveled is a great way to build the bond with your dog.

It's easier to tune out and walk the same old route every day, but by doing so you're missing out on an easy way to build exciting unpredictability into your dog's life. It's fun for dogs to take a new route and see who and what have been there, too. Varying your walk route also forces you to stay on your toes from a training perspective. When you cover the same ground the same way every day, you see a muted version of your dog's leash behavior. He knows what's around the corner, and who's been peeing on that fence post. When you open him up to new sights and smells on a different route, you get the chance to revisit some of the training basics because you'll probably be dealing with excitement pulling. ("Oh my gosh! That garbage can smells amazing! I simply must get closer to it.") That's not a bad thing, though. Leash-walking fluency, or the ability to walk politely in new environments, is an impressive skill.

Though we live on a dead-end street, I can think of at least ten different walk routes open to us. Zeke and Sumner are so used to my unpredictability (if that's not a contradiction) that they actually turn to look at me once we reach the end of the driveway to find out which way we're going on that day. They're tuned in enough so that I can point in a direction and say, "That way," and off they go. My leash-walking unpredictability is an easy way to keep them focused on me, because they never know which road we'll be traveling.

Ways to Be Fetching and Playful

A small but simple way to add some much appreciated unpredictability to your dog's life is to surprise him with play. Zeke and Sumner are aware that I might say, "Let's play a game!" at any time of day, so they realize that it's in their best interest to keep me in their sightlines. They never know when I'm going to push back from the computer and initiate a game of tug, or hide from them when they're not looking and tell them to find me (more on this great game coming up in chapter 8). Sometimes, if I find a treat in my pocket left over from my canine clients, I ask Zeke and Sum to do a quick trick like "spin!" and then go about my business. This type of unpredictability drives home the point that life with me is always interesting. They're confident of the fact that their necessities will arrive the same way every day (breakfast at seven o'clock, dinner at 4:30, quiet time after eight o'clock), but everything that comes in between is up for grabs.

Now, I'm not suggesting that in adding unpredictability you eliminate your scheduled play with your dog. If you come home from work and play fetch with him every night, more power to you! Though I maligned fetch earlier in this book, I don't think that you should abandon the game completely, because it *is* a wonderful way to exercise your dog. That said, if you think about it, fetch is a pretty boring, no-brainer kind of energy burner. Throw, retrieve, drop, throw, retrieve, drop. Ho-hum. A few simple twists can turn the game from repetitive to unpredictable, and give you yet another way to build your bond with your dog.

You scratch my back, I'll scratch yours

The easiest way to switch up your standard, everyday game of fetch is to add the "you scratch my back, I'll scratch yours" aspect. Instead of just throwing the ball for your dog, ask him to do something for you first. Keep it easy initially, and just ask him to sit before you toss the ball.

If he's not used to doing it, you might get some barky resistance. "Throw it, throw, it, throw it *now!*" If you get that reaction, drop the ball and walk away. Wait a few minutes, and then return and try again. You might have to repeat the walking away step a few times before he relents and actually does a sit for you, so don't get frustrated if it doesn't happen right away. The second his bum hits the ground, though, toss the ball. You want him to understand that sitting makes good stuff happen.

As your dog starts sitting quicker, amp it up and make him hold the sit for a few seconds before you throw the ball. When he really understands the quid pro quo nature of the game, make him work harder still. Ask him to do a down or a down-stay and walk around throwing the ball back and forth in your hands before you toss it. The beauty of incorporating basic obedience into the game is that it allows you to finesse your dog's skills while he has fun.

My client Janet was looking for a way to rev up her basic game of fetch with her Goldendoodle, Bishop. He was a pro at doing a variety of basic obedience cues and tricks before she threw the ball for him, so we decided to teach him to stay not only before the ball was thrown, but after as well. Bishop was particularly ball-crazy, so we knew we had our work cut out for us.

Janet tried it immediately after we'd discussed the concept, but before I'd laid out the specifics of how to achieve it. "Bishop, stay," she said to him solemnly. She cocked her arm back, looked down at him out of the corner of her eye, said "stay" one more time then tossed the ball. Bishop was after it before it had even left her hand.

"Well, that didn't work at all how I'd planned," she laughed.

"It's a common mistake—you're not the first!" I replied. "What usually happens when people try to teach this is they get progressively louder and more demonstrative with their stay cue. They lean down, flash their hand right in front of their dog's face and say, 'Stay,' really, really loudly. Then they throw the ball, and if they're lucky, their dog hesitates for maybe a millisecond before he takes off. The challenge is that there are so many stimulating parts to the ball-throwing process: picking up the ball, reaching back to throw it, the release. By the time you get to the actual throw, the dog is already levitating with excitement. The key is to break it down into little manageable chunks."

Always ask your dog to do something for you—like sit—before you throw the ball for him.

I put Bishop in a down-stay three steps away from me, leaned over until my hand was about a foot from the ground, and let the ball drop. Bishop quivered but managed to hold the stay. I waited a second and said, "Get it!" He'd never hear the cue before, but my tone of voice and encouraging movements toward the ball helped him understand that it was now okay for him to grab it.

"Good boy!" I made a big fuss over Bishop and looked over at Janet. She seemed unimpressed.

"That's just the first step! Don't worry, we'll get to that magnificent stay you're envisioning."

Fetch is a high-energy game. Getting your dog to settle down to do an obedience cue for you can be difficult, but don't give up!

I put Bishop back into the down-stay, stood up a little straighter, and let the ball drop. Once again, he managed to hold the stay, so I released him with the "Get it!" Feeling cocky, I put him in a down-stay five steps away from me, and then stood straight up and let the ball drop from waist height. It proved to be too much for Bishop. He headed for the ball, but I managed to intercept the steal by covering the ball with my foot before he got to it.

"That was trainer error—he wasn't ready for that step yet. The foot trick was to keep him from rewarding himself for getting up—do that any time you see him moving to get the ball before you've said 'Get it.' It's a great little trick during the early teaching stages of the process."

Janet raced through the initial steps with Bishop. I was pleased to see that he was more responsive with her than he was with me.

If you're wondering why I wasn't using treats for this, here's why: I actually don't like using treats for fetch and toy stuff if the dog is motivated by the game itself. There's no need to—the game is reinforcing enough.

Janet progressed to gently tossing the ball a foot away from her. Bishop even managed to look away from the ball and toward Janet's face, waiting for the "Get it" cue. For her final throw, she tossed it two feet away and then waited three seconds before she released Bishop to grab it. He nailed it! We were quite impressed with ourselves that day.

Magic-ball fetch

Since this chapter is all about keeping life unpredictable for your dog, why not shake up his very belief in what fetch means? He probably understands that fetch involves tossing a ball, chasing after it, and then some variation of giving it back to you. (That depends on how well you've trained the drop, of course!) How interesting would life be for your dog if you threw the ball and then it kept moving around unpredictably—and he couldn't actually catch it? All you need is a standard tennis ball and a long length of thin rope (fifteen feet is a good start). Use a knife or scissors to pierce the ball on either side. Slip the string through both holes and tie it tightly around the ball. Wrap the string up so that you can comfortably carry it, grab a second tennis ball, and call your dog.

Making a ball on a string is easy—and it's a great way to add some unpredictability to your basic game of fetch.

Go through your regular routine of asking your dog to do something for you before you throw the "magic" ball, and then toss it as far as the rope will allow. As soon as your dog gets close to it, jerk the rope so that the ball moves. (Yes, you have to have good reflexes to make it work.) Let your dog chase the ball and grab it, and then play a little tug with it. Reel your dog in and get him to drop the magic ball. Make a show of winding the rope back up, turn your back, switch to the non-magic ball (the one not on a string), and give it a toss. From that point on, Fido will never know if he's going to get the standard, everyday ball, or the chase-able, tug-able one!

The magic ball is also a great way to motivate dogs who don't love the game of fetch. Instead of tossing the ball off into the distance, let it land right in front of your dog, and then tug it enticingly in front of him. Few dogs can resist something rolling past their feet!

Rapid-fire fetch

The final game that you can add to your fetch arsenal to keep the game unpredictable for your dog is rapid-fire fetch. This version of the game requires that you're in decent shape as well, because you'll need to dash around collecting balls with your dog. Round up at least five of the same type of balls. You want them to be equal for your dog so that he isn't fixated on just one of them. Take him to an open space, ask him to do an easy obedience cue for you, and then toss the first ball. This will be the only time he'll have to do a cue for you, because the object of this fetch game is speed. Praise him as he heads back to you with the ball. I say, "Bring it!" in a cheerful voice to my guys when they're approaching with a ball. The "Bring it" cue has become strong enough with my guys just through that type of casual usage to allow me to tell them to "bring it" if they start to veer off course on the way to bringing a ball to me or if something catches their attention and they "forget" that I'm waiting for the ball.

When your dog is about a foot away from you, tell him "Drop," and, the moment he releases the ball, quickly throw a new ball for him in a different direction. Be obvious about changing the direction of the throw, because he might be conditioned to run in the same direction all the time. Collect the original ball while he's retrieving the new one. Repeat the process when he gets close to you with the second ball, throwing yet another ball in a completely new direction. Time the drop cue so that he's close enough to you that you can easily collect the ball after he drops it. Throw the balls more quickly each time, always changing the direction of your toss, so that he's racing back and forth wildly trying to corral the balls. This is an intense, fast-paced version of the predictable fetch game, and it's guaranteed to tax even the most seasoned fetcher!

There's more to fetch than toss and retrieve!

Dogs Cannot Live by Biscuits Alone

The dry dog-biscuit marketing team has done its job, because for some reason much of the American public is convinced that dry dog biscuits are exactly what dogs want. My unofficial field research points to different results. Dogs will eat dry biscuits, certainly—but, given a choice, they'll select something moist and meaty over the biscuit every time. There are endless treat options available, so why bore your dog's palate with the same old, same old when you want to pay him for a job well done? Adding unpredictability to your dog's reward choices is yet another simple, effective way to remind him that you make the good stuff happen!

I always have a variety of store-bought treats available for Zeke and Sumner, and I supplement those with an array of surprising goodies that keeps them guessing. They never know if they're going to get a meaty store-bought dog treat, a morsel of sliced American cheese, a bit of pretzel, or, sometimes, a piece of apple. Though I'm treat-crazy, I never dole them out without getting something in return. Zeke and Sumner know that there's no such thing as free lunch in our house!

Keep meals predictable

Unpredictability can touch many aspects of your dog's life, but his meals shouldn't be one of them. Switching foods without allowing for the proper transition time—usually about a week—can lead to intestinal distress. (That's a nice way of saying that your dog will have runny poo.)

Experiment and try to figure out what treat types your dog prefers. Is he a liver fanatic or a cheese-aholic? (*Note:* Too much cheese can be a bad thing for dogs.) Figure out your dog's "hierarchy" of treats. Your dog may adore pretzels when he's working with you around your house, but that same treat might be as good as dirt when you're trying to work with him during a distraction-filled walk.

Treats are not the only reward options available to you. "Real-life" rewards are equally powerful for increasing your dog's responsiveness and attentiveness. One of the most common complaints I hear from my clients is that their dogs are hesitant to perform behaviors if they know that they're not going to get paid with a treat. Treats are vitally important during the initial training process, but your dog shouldn't hold his responses for ransom if you don't have a treat on you. Using real-life rewards helps to lessen your dog's dependency on food payments; plus, it keeps him guessing about what you're going to do next.

My client David admitted that he was frustrated with training. We were on the third lesson (out of six), and he felt like his English Springer Spaniel, Kaya, was "blowing him off." She didn't want to work if she figured out that he didn't have a treat in his pocket. "She knows how to do the basics, but if I don't have a treat, she won't do anything!" he complained.

I told him, "Don't worry, this is a typical concern. You've been really generous about giving Kaya treats, which is a good thing at this stage. Now we want to slowly begin weaning her off her dependence on treats by teaching her that the treats are going to come sporadically. Sometimes, instead of getting a treat, she'll get something else that she wants."

"But she doesn't want anything *but* treats—that's the problem!" David laughed.

"Oh, you'd be surprised. I think that there are plenty of things that she wants from you that you could use as rewards. She likes to be brushed, right?"

"Definitely. She brings me the brush sometimes!"

"Okay, then, there's another reward option for you. Let's say you ask her to do an easy inside recall, and when she gets to you, instead of giving her a treat you break out the brush that you'd been hiding in your back pocket and give her a quick once over. Then on the next recall, give her a little piece of cheese that you've hidden up on the shelf. She thought that you didn't have food but—surprise!—you did. On the final recall, go back to the brushing, and then finish up the exercise with some calming massage. Switch it up. That way she'll never know what you're going to offer her next."

"I can do that. It requires more planning, but I guess it's worth it," David said.

"Once you start thinking about new ways to reward Kaya, you won't be able to stop. I just thought of another one, as a matter of fact. You know that big patch of ivy that she loves to run through? Instead of just letting her take off and play in it, have her hold a stay while you walk to the end of the leash. Then release her and run over to it with her."

"That makes sense. I can use a round of tug as a reward as well," he said.

"Now you get what I'm talking about. Treats are most dogs' first-choice reward, but there are so many other options out there!"

Say What?

Adding inconsistency to your dog's daily life is an easy way to help your dog figure out that you're creative and fun to be around. It gives your dog a reason to tune in to you. It changes your dog's perspective from "Oh, *you* again" to "What are you going to do next?!" Yes, dogs thrive on a schedule, but your bond will thrive if you surprise your dog with a little unpredictability every day!

Chapter 7

BUILDING BLOCK #3: PRAISE!

talk to my dog while we walk. Is that okay? I tell her what a good job she's doing, and how happy I am with her walking."

A few of my clients sheepishly admit this to me as if they're embarrassed. Somehow it seems odd to praise a dog for doing exactly what she should be doing in the first place—walking politely. But why is there guilt in acknowledging a job well done?

Unfortunately, not all of my clients are effusive praisers. In fact, most of them are far from it—their dogs exist in a "praise vacuum." I cajole praise out of them when their dogs do something worthy, and even then the praise is muted and dull. I have yet to figure out why. After all, praise is free, it's easy, and it's always accessible. Praise is a simple way to strengthen your bond with your dog *hundreds* of time each day.

Praise comes easily for the miraculous and impressive, like the jaw-dropping recall your dog performed instead of chasing after a rabbit, or the poetic Frisbee-catch she just executed. It doesn't flow as easily for the basic stuff that she does every day, like sitting before you put on her leash or peeing in the proper spot. You *expect* her to do those things for you—they're givens, after all—so you think that there's no need to acknowledge them. However, praising your dog is yet another straightforward way to strengthen your bond, because it lets your dog know that you appreciate her when she listens to you.

A few years ago, I noticed a praise deficit in myself, but it wasn't with my canine clients. I discovered that, although I heap kudos on my furry students, I was accidentally refraining from encouraging my *human* students for their efforts! I'm reformed, and I now recognize the two-legged side of the training equation every time they accomplish something during the session, even if it's only a well-timed click. Granted, in some households, I have to struggle to find something praise-worthy ("You did *one* session of homework last week—that's better than none. Awesome!"), but most of my clients now hear a stream of "Perfect. That was *fantastic*. Perfect. Perfect!" during our session. Once you start looking for behaviors to praise, it's difficult to *stop* seeing them!

The sad fact is that most of us don't praise enough. It's easy to dole it out to a cute young pup just learning the ropes, but we get lax with it as our dogs mature. It's probably because we become complacent with our dogs' daily behavior—three walks a day multiplied over a lifetime equals a lot of monotony and seemingly little behavior worthy of notice. How wrong we are! There are small miracles in so many daily moments with our dogs, and by acknowledging them, we not only strengthen our relationships, we set our dogs up to want to perform the behavior again. Praising your dog helps her to understand what's "right," it shows her what behaviors you appreciate, and it encourages her to listen to you. More important, it shows her that the good stuff that she does every day matters to you!

So when should you praise your dog?

Any time she does something that you like and that you'd like her to repeat. Once you start doing it, you'll be surprised to discover how many opportunities you have to praise your dog every day. Let's get to the specifics.

Bathroom Behavior

Pottying outside is a much appreciated but overlooked canine behavior. It's the given of all givens, since most of us couldn't tolerate a dog who eliminated inside the house instead of out. (I say "most," because, believe it or not, I get many pained inquiries from people who do just that for years.) Your dog eliminates outside numerous times a day, so why not let her know that it's an excellent behavior that you'd like to see her continue?

I make a habit of praising Zeke and Sumner for pottying while we're on walks, particularly when they use good "toiletiquette" and pick a telephone pole over a neighbor's mailbox. I always praise my clients' dogs when they potty during a walk, and I inevitably get a look from the dog that seems to say "*Really?* You like this?" I quietly acknowledge while the dog is in the act ("Very nice, good job") and then do so effusively after she finishes ("Nice work!"). When I'm walking my dogs, I give effusive kudos when they opt to poop close to the garbage can so I don't have to carry the bag with me for the entire walk. They both now time their bombs so that I can scoop and then toss them right away!

My client Kay adopted a young rescue dog, Roscoe, who needed help polishing up his outdoor potty skills. (Peeing *in* the house? He had that one covered.) Kay was a lovely praiser during the first part of our lesson, so I knew she wouldn't have a problem praising Roscoe for pottying in the yard to further reinforce the behavior. We took a potty break after the first few training exercises, and Kay waited patiently while Roscoe looked for just the right spot. The *second* he tucked himself into the universal pooping position, Kay whooped, "*Good* Roscoe! Good, good, *good!* Good boy! Good potty!" Her praise was so passionate that it startled Roscoe, and he tried to move away from her, dropping poop nuggets behind him as she trilled. Kay was so good at praising that I was hesitant to say anything, but I could see that the potty praises-interruptus would curtail the housetraining process.

"Kay, I love how you praise Roscoe," I told her. "But it looks like you'll need to alter your approach when it comes to pottying. You should praise Roscoe quietly while he goes, but hold off on the loud boisterous stuff until

> ## Pay on delivery
>
> Having trouble with housetraining? It helps to give your dog a tasty treat immediately after she finishes pottying. You're not rewarding the *act* of elimination, you're rewarding the *location.* You're telling her, "When you go out here, you get paid!"

he's completely done. Big-time praise often makes dogs stop before the chamber is empty, particularly when it comes to urine. Because you're also giving Roscoe a treat when he finishes, he'll probably assume that your praise means that he should go to you to collect his paycheck. Then you'll wind up taking him inside when he still has more to do. Or he'll freak out, as he just did."

At our final potty trip of the lesson, Kay took my advice to heart and quietly chanted, "Good Roscoe, good job" while he eliminated, and then amped it up the moment he finished. Roscoe seemed to appreciate the change in intensity.

Walking

Now let's assume that you put my advice from chapter 5 into practice, and your dog is beginning to understand that walking close to you is a very good thing. She's getting treats every so often, but she should also be getting loads of verbal encouragement to go along with them. You'll be *slowly* phasing out the treats over time, but praise for a job well done should never stop. I'm not suggesting that you resort to a nonstop stream of "Nice work! So good! That was exceptional. Good girl!" type of praise, but a well-timed "Hi, sweetie!" when she chooses to glance up at you can do wonders. Imagine what a *huge* compliment it is when your dog looks up at your face instead of focusing on the temptations around you. Meeting her gaze with a smile and a heartfelt word of praise gives her valuable feedback: "He likes this! *This* I can do!"

Praising your dog also reinforces the idea that walking is a united adventure. Taking note of the appropriate things your dog does during a walk is good for her, but it's also good for *you* because it keeps you engaged in the process. Forcing yourself to focus on your dog and occasionally praise her for good behavior prohibits you from disconnecting from the experience—you can't chat on the cellphone and praise her at the same time. In order to acknowledge the small yet important moments that happen during the average walk, you need to be invested in the process, and that means, yes, paying attention.

I don't encourage the slavish, show-dog type of attention that wows 'em at Westminster, where the dog sticks right to her handler's leg and rarely looks away from the person's face. Walks are recreational for both you and your dog, and it's silly to think that your dog can enjoy her walk if she's forced to stay glued to your side and not have the opportunity to sniff the world. My definition of a good leash walk is one where your dog picks a side of your body and remains close and attentive to you but still has the freedom to stop and check out who has been peeing on her favorite bush. Anything that happens within those parameters—keeping the leash slack, pace similar, and glancing up every so often—should be acknowledged with occasional words of encouragement.

I do a great deal of praising my dogs when we walk, so much so that I often wonder if my neighbors think I'm crazy. I recently got busted by a car full of teenagers as I walked down the street, praising Zeke in my typically silly way. I thought we were alone on the street, so I let Zeke know how phenomenal he was as he walked beside me. "You're looking good, mister," I said. "So fancy today! You're a little high-stepper. *Very* nice!" As I got closer to the car, I noticed that the windows were down, and the kids had heard every goofy word.

Give your dog encouragement when she looks up at you during a walk—it's a compliment!

A typical segment of our walk might look and sound like this: Zeke veers out to sniff a telephone pole but manages to get all his sniffing done quickly and catches up to me right after I pass. "Good job, Zeke, nice work," I say as he's walking next to me. Sumner hears barking in the distance, perks up, and then immediately looks back at me to make sure everything is still okay. "Good boy, Sum. No worries. Noooo worries!" I want him to know that he made the right decision when he looked at me instead of freaking out about the dog in the distance. The three of us walk for a long stretch with our paces similar. Zeke and Sum are a few steps ahead of me but in tandem. Their leashes are curved. "Nice work, guys," I tell them. Zeke looks up at me, and I give him a smile.

I always remind my clients that they should praise their dogs as they walk, only to have them halfheartedly muster up a self-conscious "Good, good." I realize that it can be embarrassing to praise your dog just for strolling along beside you during a walk, particularly if your neighbors are out. Ignore them! Upbeat approval during a walk is a surefire way to let your dog know that you like her style. The more you tell her, the more often she'll choose to do it.

Recall Approach

Aaron, his dog Monroe, and I were halfway through lesson number one. We were working on the basic recall, and though the introductory exercise was simple, Monroe was acting as if he had to cross broken glass to get to Aaron. His responses to Aaron's "here" were tentative.

"Aaron," I suggested, "the next time you call Monroe, as soon as he looks over his shoulder at you, tell him he's a good boy. Praise him a little."

He nodded his head. Aaron called to him, and Monroe swung his head toward him.

"Good boy," Aaron said tentatively.

"More!" I whispered, not wanting to break Monroe's concentration. "More encouragement!"

"Good job, Monroe! Atta boy!"

Monroe turned all the way toward Aaron, which elicited additional praise from him. Aaron saw his dog's attitude shifting. I had a hunch that Monroe had been punished for not coming fast enough, so we were attempting to undo some damage during the initial recall lesson. The praise was new for Monroe, but it looked like he was getting over some of his recall issues and getting into the game. "Good boy!"

Monroe broke into a trot. "Good job! Good!" Aaron encouraged.

"Give him lots of praise when he gets to you," I called out. "This is a pretty big improvement over the last response you got."

Monroe cantered the last leg to Aaron and was rewarded with a treat, a chest scratch, and effusive praise.

"There you go!" I beamed. "See how praising Monroe's initial interest in you encouraged him to speed up? Awesome work!"

We practiced a few more times, and each attempt saw Monroe picking up speed and getting more excited about the game. Aaron's praise grew more effusive with each repetition. Success!

Many of my clients note that when I call their dogs during the recall exercise, the dogs usually race to me much more quickly than they go to them. Part of the reason is because I represent only good things to dogs: treats, play, and positive attention. The other reason is because I always encourage a speedy recall by praising the dogs as they're running to me. Rather than sitting silently when a dog turns to look at me, I tell her that she's got the right idea by saying something like, "*Very* nice! Good job!" I throw in some whistling or kissy noises and I continue praising as the dog crosses the room to me. I always finish up with more praise when she arrives at my feet.

Praising your dog as she begins coming to you can also turn a questionable recall into a definite one. If you call your dog and she turns to look at you and then stops, she's weighing her options. Help her make up her mind by praising even the *idea* of returning to you. She's looking at you—praise her for that attention! Once she's committed to coming to you, show your approval by continuing the praise party.

Praise becomes particularly important when you move the recall outside. Not only are you competing with the environmental distractions, but you've probably also increased the distance between you and your dog when you call her. Stack the deck in your favor and praise her joyfully as she returns to you!

Everyday Obedience

Asking your dog to sit before you put on her leash or before you toss a ball for her will become second nature for both of you—you won't even have to think about it. The part that you *should* think about is praising your dog for responding to you. It doesn't get more basic than this, folks. You ask your dog to do something, she does it, and then you praise her for it. A simple but heartfelt "Good job!" is your "Thank you" to your dog's "Please."

Mind your manners

Asking you dog to "say please" is an excellent way to incorporate basic obedience into your everyday life. She wants you to throw the ball? Ask her to "say please" by sitting first. She wants out? Ask her to "say please" by sitting first instead of scratching at the door. And don't forget to praise her when she does it!

That speedy smiling sit deserves praise.

Checking In

You're at the dog park and your dog dashes up to you. What do you do? Give her an absentminded ear scratch and keep talking to the person standing next to you? Ignore her completely? I certainly hope not. Your dog checking in with you when she's off-leash is one of the greatest compliments she can pay you. She's choosing to stop playing, chasing, or sniffing and make contact with *you*. That's huge—and worthy of your acknowledgement. A simple, "Nice work!" when she runs over to you is an easy way to encourage the behavior to happen again. (What's rewarded will be repeated.)

Nobody understood that point better than my client Joe. He lived on a large, tree-filled property with his gorgeous black Lab, Rex. The property was fenced, so there was no worry that Rex could slip out, but Joe occasionally had trouble getting Rex to come back to him when he was running free. Joe knew that chasing Rex to try to get him back was a losing proposition (four legs trump two), so he asked me to help him address the behavior.

We worked on the many different recall exercises until Rex was responding like a pro both inside and outside. As Rex's recall became stronger, we spent more of our lessons outside on Joe's property, strolling and chatting in between each practice session. Rex spent much of his off-duty time flexing

Praising your dog for checking in with you will encourage her to do it more often.

his squirrel-chasing muscles. Each time Rex finished a hunt, he'd return to me with a wiggle and a grin. "Atta boy," I'd tell him. "You really showed that squirrel who's boss!"

I looked over at Joe. "Do you see how Rex keeps checking in with me after he's done chasing squirrels? That's what I want him to start doing with you. His recall is getting really strong, which is great, but on a property like this, that's not enough. He's got plenty of room to roam and tons of stuff to keep him busy out here. It's important that he finds value in you as well, even when faced with all the temptations out here. I want him to *want* to keep tabs on you and check in with you, even if you didn't call him over."

"So should I give him a treat every time he comes near me?" Joe asked.

"Yes, rewarding him with food will definitely help, but I also want you to connect with him and really praise him as well. Make a big fuss as he's running toward you, and then give him some love when he's right at your feet. Remember, you're not *calling* him to come to you, you're just acknowledging him when he *chooses* to do it on his own. There's a big difference between the two. With a recall he's responding to a cue, but with a check-in he's doing so just because he *wants* to connect with you. He's certainly allowed to run around and enjoy your property, though. I'm not suggesting that he has to stay glued to you the whole time you're out here. . . . I just want him to want to know where you are, that's all."

Rex had been walking near us as we talked but caught sight of a daring squirrel at the base of a tree and took off.

Joe watched him thoughtfully. The moment Rex finished his pursuit and started back toward us, Joe shouted, "You got 'em, Rexie! Good job!"

That was all it took. Rex bounded to us as if the commendation from his most favorite person in the world had given him a caffeine jolt. I stayed quiet while Joe hooted and hollered his appreciation for Rex's speedy return. "Good job, Rexie! Good boy! Aren't you a handsome hunter!" Joe reached down, gave Rex a small treat, and scratched him behind the ears.

"See? You didn't call him to come to you, but you did acknowledge him for choosing to come back to you. Let's keep this up."

We continued walking and chatting. Rex alternated between walking close to us and darting off each time he heard a rustling in the trees. Joe managed to carry on his conversation with me and still dole out praise each time Rex checked in with him. "Such a good boy," he'd say, smiling at Rex when he came over and checked in.

Suddenly we heard a tremendous crashing in the distance. The three of us stopped in our tracks. Rex's nose twitched, and he took off after what we now could see was a young buck.

"There's a dip in the fence and they manage to jump it." Joe said to me, his brow furrowed. "This is going to be a tough one. Rex has only seen one other deer this close and it took him an hour to stop obsessing about the scent trail. I couldn't catch him, and he wouldn't come to me. It was a nightmare."

"Well, hopefully things have changed since we've been doing all this practice with Rex over the past few weeks," I said. "Let's follow behind him and see what happens."

The buck had managed to jump back over the fence and was nowhere to be seen, but, as Joe had predicted, Rex was furiously circling over the deer's tracks. He was a dog possessed. Even so, Rex managed to look up at us and acknowledge us as we approached. Joe immediately said, "Nice work, buddy! You told him where to go!" Rex looked up at Joe and wagged his tail in agreement. "Good boy! What a good boy you are," Joe said. We stood and watched Rex inhaling the ground for a few moments.

"Okay, let's turn and walk away," I said to Joe. "We're not going to call him to come with us, though. Let's see what happens."

We began walking, and it didn't take long for Rex to catch up with us. Joe was surprised by the response, but ready. He gave Rex a treat and commenced with the party. "There's my guy! Look at my little hunter! *Good* boy, Rex. Good boy!" Joe seemed so shocked and pleased by Rex's decision to follow us and leave the deer tracks behind that the praise he lavished on Rex was more genuine and heartfelt than any I'd seen. Rex looked proud of himself and wagged his whole body. I wished that I had captured their beautiful interaction on film so that I could show it to all my clients. Joe wrote the book on praise!

Responsiveness at that level doesn't always happen quickly, though. Joe already had an excellent relationship with his dog, so the check-ins came more naturally for Rex, and they happened even in highly distracting environments. Joe had been working on his bond with Rex in other scenarios, so Rex already knew that his person was fun, unpredictable, and rewarding. Joe's praising when Rex checked in helped to make that bond even stronger, and encouraged Rex to do it more often, even in the face of tempting distractions like the buck.

Stopping Naughty Behavior

"Can I say 'no' to my dog?"

Since I'm all about positive, dog-friendly training, I get that question all the time. Clients understand the concept of rewarding good behavior, but they're not sure what to do about stopping inappropriate behavior. I'm not a big fan of using the word *no,* because we tend to say it all the time, to the point where it almost becomes part of the dog's name. My client Krista told me a funny story that illustrated the point: A visiting nephew turned to her and asked if her dog Polly's full name was actually "Paulino." Confused, she asked why.

"Because you keep calling her that!"

It took Krista a few minutes to figure out that her perceptive nephew had caught her saying "Polly, no!" over and over again.

Instead of using the word *no,* I try to teach the dog not to engage in the unwanted behavior to begin with. Instead of saying, "No, Scout, no!" when she jumps on guests, I teach her to respond to the arm-cross sit instead. Instead of shouting "No" at her when she grabs a sneaker, I make sure that the house is dog-proofed and she has a variety of desirable chews. That said, there are instances where some sort of "Don't do that" marker needs to be used. The new puppy who considers digging in the potted plant could use some sort of verbal discouragement. I prefer to use a guttural sound like "eh eh" to a let a dog know that she's about to do something inappropriate.

There's a missing link to this behavior, though. You guessed it: praise.

David was a phenomenal new puppy owner. He had all his bases covered before I even showed up for our first lesson, from crate training to housetraining, to the nipping and the jumping up. It was clear that he'd done his homework and was doing a phenomenal job with his Brittany Spaniel, Harley. "You're perfect!" I told him. "I'm so impressed!"

He even knew about the "eh eh." As we chatted, he spotted Harley chewing on the fringe of his Oriental rug. "Eh eh," he said. She stopped and looked at him, and then went back to chewing on the fringe. "Eh eh," he said. Once again, she paused for a moment and then went back to chewing. David started to "Eh" one more time and I stopped him. "Let me give her a bone."

Praise your pup when you catch her playing with one of her toys.

"Okay, you're *almost* perfect," I said as I walked back to my chair. "You kept her from chewing on the rug the right way, but you forgot to praise her."

"Praise her for what?"

"When you said 'eh eh,' she stopped what she was doing, right? She listened to you." He nodded. "Well, then tell her she's a good girl! Praise her for stopping! It feels really counterintuitive, doesn't it? She shouldn't be chewing on the fringe in the first place, so why in the world are we praising her for stopping doing something we don't want her to do? Well, first of all, she doesn't know that she's not supposed to be chewing on the carpet—that's what puppy-proofing is for! That said, we should praise her because she *did* stop. You'll find that if you praise her after you ask her to stop doing something, she'll be more likely to stop quicker in the future. It's weird, I know. Don't worry, we'll have another opportunity to practice it over the next hour, and I'll show you what I mean."

Sure enough, when we sat down at the end of the lesson to go over homework, punchy Harley started absentmindedly chewing at the chair leg beneath David.

"Eh eh!" I said to her. She stopped chewing and looked at me. "Good girl, Harley! What a good little girl you are!" With that she got up and wiggled over to me. I gave her a bone and the leg-chewing crisis was averted.

"See what happened? If I had just said 'eh eh' and ignored her, I guarantee that she would've gone back to chewing on the chair leg. Because I praised her for stopping and gave her the chew, she abandoned it."

The next week when I showed up, it was clear that the lesson had sunk in. Harley was nosing around the edge of the low coffee table, trying to grab the remote control. David said "Eh eh!" and then immediately followed up with effusive praise when Harley stopped and looked at him. He walked over to where she stood, gave her a chew, and put the remote on a high shelf. "My fault: incomplete puppy-proofing," he said with a shrug.

I've found that this forgotten praise opportunity gets amazing results. I continue to do it with Zeke and Sumner to this day, though my "eh eh" has morphed into a lighthearted "Don't even think about it."

Take a knee

A punchy puppy is usually overtired. Puppies don't always know when to stop playing and take a break, so if your puppy is biting, jumping up, or grabbing contraband and won't stop, it's a good idea to give her some crate time to relax. Take her out for a potty break, and then give her a chew or activity toy in her crate. She'll probably fall asleep quickly!

For example, I'm prepping dinner and a big sliver of onion falls on the ground in front of Zeke's feet. He starts to move toward it. "Don't even think about it," I say. He settles into a down right next to it and immediately gets big love from me. "That was great, Roundie! Thanks!"

Sumner's ears prick up when he hears the detested neighbor dog walk close to the fence. "Don't even think about it." He turns to look at me, weighing his options, and I give him a smile. "So good! Very nice, Summie! Let's go!" Withdrawing his attention from the neighbor dog for even a moment is worthy of praise (she's that big of a distraction), so I make sure to time my acknowledgement correctly. That's enough to get him to come along with me, thereby avoiding yet another battle royale.

How to Praise

You've thought about giving your dog more praise, and you're committed to giving it a shot. But what does that mean, exactly? What type of praise is best? How much is enough? Welcome to yet another opportunity to learn to speak dog.

Much like petting, you'll need to watch your dog to see how she responds to your praise. Some dogs enjoy high-pitched, boisterous praise; others find that type of acknowledgement off-putting. The dog who is enjoying high-pitched praise will stay close and continue wiggling and responding to the

---

Say my name

"Roundie"? I know I'm not the only one who has a few million bizarre nicknames for my dogs. His original nickname was "Roundface Pink Belly Boy" because he does indeed have a round head and a very pink belly. That evolved into "Round" and "Roundie." Sumner is known as "The Prince," "Princie McPrince," and "Phat Sum."

I christen my canine clients with a nickname during our sessions (usually "Gorgeous," "Sweetie," or "Cutie"), because I've found that people overuse their dogs' proper names until they become the equivalent of verbal wallpaper. I want my canine students to know that I'll only use their proper names if I absolutely, 100 percent need them to focus on me. When that time comes and the dog hears me say, "Scout!" for the first time, you can guarantee that she's going to turn around and see what warranted the change in name. The problem is that I become so used to using the nickname that I often forget the dog's real name!

affirmation from her owner. The dog who doesn't might put her ears back, duck her head, or move away from her owner. I've found that squeaky praise tends to make dogs either anxious or over-excited. Many dogs respond to that type of boisterous praise by jumping and getting revved up. If you're running your dog through an agility course, that's a fine reaction. If you're trying to take a quick potty walk before you leave for work, or acknowledge your dog for sitting instead of leaping on your granny, it's probably not the best idea.

Some dogs take praise and run with it, literally. When I praise Sumner during a leash walk, he tends to speed up, as if to say, "You like this walking? I can do more of it, and faster! Watch me!" I've noticed the speeding-up behavior with my canine clients as well. I still praise these jolly dogs, but I do so quietly in an effort to avoid the "praise pride" effect.

My praise tends to be more chatty and conversational in tone. I opt to use multisyllabic words like *fantastic, wonderful,* and, my favorite, *excellent* (or, as I say it, "*Ex*-cellent!") I don't just say "good," I give a short, encouraging narrative description of what just went on, in a low but still upbeat tone. "Hello, gorgeous! That was fantastic! Look how fast you are! You are *so* clever!" That could be a waste of words, but the dogs don't seem to mind! Their reactions are uniformly happy and appropriate, with minimal jumping up and hyperactivity. My body is loose and playful when I praise, and I tend to crouch down as I do it to prevent them from jumping up.

Dogs appreciate different types of praise.

Facial expressions play a role in praise as well. It's nearly impossible to give heartfelt praise without lapsing into some sort of happy expression. I defy you to joyfully exclaim, "What a good dog!" with a straight face. Dogs recognize our facial expressions, from the furrowed brow to the welcoming grin. (Here's a test to prove my point: The next time your dog looks at you, say nothing, but smile at her. Expect a tail wag in response, or more.) Proper praise engages not only your voice, but your posture and demeanor as well.

Men tend to have a tougher time engaging the entire "praise trinity" of proper tone, facial expression, and posture. A memorable exception was my client Jake, a big bear of a man. He managed to praise his Boxer, Red, with a playfulness that made my heart sing. When he praised, his tone went up so that his naturally deep voice took on a gentler pitch. He probably recognized that he sounded silly, so the smile that played on his face, from his eyebrows to his mouth, made it clear that he was in on the joke and that he was enjoying himself. He downplayed his size by bending over or kneeling when he praised Red. His dedication to appropriate praising always made my day!

Heartfelt praise is the easiest of the bond-building tips. It doesn't require planning, it's easy, it's effective, and you always have the necessary tool with you! Effective praising doesn't require a personality transplant—you don't have to develop a syrupy tone and a perpetually sunny disposition in order to make it work. It's simple to say "Nice work" when your dog takes a pee break or "Good job," when she executes a well-timed sit. The opportunities to praise your dog are limitless once you begin paying attention. Now's a great time to start!

Chapter 8

BUILDING BLOCK #4: PLAYING TO WIN

Want to fast-track the bonding process with your dog? Play with him. I'm not talking about absent-minded games of fetch while you talk on the phone or watch TV. Bond-building play comes about when you apply creativity and a joyful spirit to the game—you have to be an active participant in it. Play shouldn't be a chore, or a way to check "burn energy" off your dog's daily to-do list. Having a good time with your dog through uninhibited pant-inducing play is yet another way to drive home the point that you bring the fun. While a walk around the neighborhood is a great start, play is the best way to exhaust your dog, both mentally and physically. And who can argue that a tired dog is a good dog?

I divide play into two camps: body games and brain games. Think of the difference between chess and football. While there is some crossover between the games (the maneuvering on a football field can be equated to a large-scale game of chess), one calls for brain and the other calls for brawn. Body games

Do you have a play-aversive dog?

You can certainly encourage a love of play, but keep in mind that *training* a dog to fetch or tug is something entirely different from uncovering an untapped love of the game. Much like you can train a dog to sit when you ask, you can also train him to retrieve a ball or pull on a rope toy when you ask. But is he enjoying the game, or just playing to earn a reward in exchange for the ball? Helping a dog discover the joy of object-based play isn't the same thing as training a behavior like sit or down. Dogs should play for the fun of the game, not because it's expected of them. So how do you uncover a love of play? I've found that most dogs can't resist a rapidly retreating object, so a ball on a string, moving enticingly along the ground is a good place to start!

are like football and engage the whole of the dog. (Yes that includes the brain, but to a lesser degree!) The body games require strength, speed and agility. The brain games require a creative, curious mind but don't call for as much "intensity." Both types of games are beneficial, but I like the brain games a bit more because they're suitable for dogs of all ages (even slow-moving senior dogs, or dogs recovering from injuries), you don't need much space for them, and they require creativity from both players. That said, nothing wears out a punchy dog like a few creative body games!

Play is an all-encompassing topic – countless books have been written on the subject. Play options run the gamut from dog sports like agility and herding to "busy" toys manufactured to tax a dog's brain. While this list isn't exclusive, I've found the following games to be easy, effective bond builders.

The Body Games

Tug

Are you ambivalent about playing tug? I always ask my clients if they mind my playing tug with their dog, and many pause before they grant permission. The myth that tug is a "gateway drug" that will turn your dog from a companion to a competitor is pervasive. Tug has the unfortunate reputation that it can "make your dog aggressive" or "become Alpha." I'm not sure I understand how that could happen, though. You play a few rounds of tug and suddenly your dog is sitting at the head of the table and using your checkbook? Tug is a wonderful bond-building game that just needs an image overhaul.

Don't believe the hype: Tug is a great, dog-friendly energy burner!

Keep 'em special

Rather than leave your dog's toys strewn around the room or piled up in a corner, put them in a spot where your dog can't get to them. A toy that gets stepped over every day loses its appeal quickly, but a toy that's kept up in the closet and only comes out when you want to engage in play remains intriguing. Another benefit? You become the magical toy dispenser. When you're around, toys come out to play!

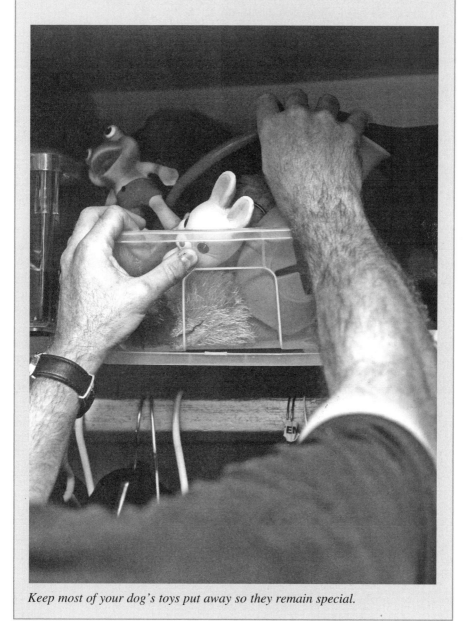

Keep most of your dog's toys put away so they remain special.

How do I love tug? Let me count the ways:

- **It's a "connected" game.** Unlike fetch, the entire game revolves around you and your dog interacting at close range, typically no more than a few feet apart. (That could be the very reason that tug is off-putting for many people. The passionate head-shaking intensity of the game brings out the dog in most dogs.)
- **You don't need a massive yard or house to play the game effectively.** In fact, you could probably play a pant-inducing game of tug in the confines of the average bathroom!
- **It's a great energy zapper.** Tug involves more than just latching on to the toy and not letting go. A proper game begins with an invitation to play and a variety of training cues including "take," "wait," and "drop." Frequent breaks for training also help to flesh out the game and burn some of that mental energy. Though I classify tug as a body game, a few tweaks and you've engaged the brain as well!
- **Tug is an effective training reward.** I always encourage people to use play as a reward in addition to, or in place of, treats. That said, play can be difficult to incorporate into some training scenarios. You can't break out a ball for a quick game of fetch during a leash walk to reward a block's worth of polite walking, but you *can* pull out a tug toy and engage in a few moments of play as you walk together.

Everything I know about tug I learned from Zeke. He's mad for the game. He loves to fetch, but because of his preference, most games of fetch devolve into tugging. I allow the shift because his hips pay the price after too much fetching, and tug enables him to burn energy without overly taxing his aging body. He can essentially stand in one spot and safely tug to his heart's content.

A proper game of tug involves more than offering your dog an object and holding on for the ride. There are a few important rules that must be in place for effective, safe tugging:

- Rule #1: You begin the game with "take."
- Rule #2: Your dog knows how to drop and wait when you ask.
- Rule #3: You take frequent training breaks.

So what do you tug with? I've seen everything from socks to old dishrags used as tug toys, but the best tug toy is one that was manufactured for that purpose. Your dog can't decipher between the cast-off socks you've designated for tug and the ones that are awaiting the washing machine, so only use real dog toys for play. I've found that most dogs prefer a soft tug toy that gives slightly over the hard plastic kind. The softer toys are easier on the teeth as well!

Zeke loves to play tug—and he's good at it!

Rule #1: Begin the game with "take"

Remember Wanda and her bossy, fetch-obsessed dog Misha (see chapter 2)? The first rule of tug is an attempt to avoid just that sort of behavior. It's important for your dog to understand that *you* determine when the game begins, as well as when it ends. Teaching him to take when you ask is a very clear way to signal when you're ready to play. The "take" cue also prevents pushy, grabby behavior when you're trying to find the least sloppy end of the toy to grasp. Zeke had the unpleasant habit of latching on to the toy and beginning the game before I was actually ready, which often led to my shoulder getting wrenched. Since I taught him to "take" he knows to wait patiently while I adjust my grip and steel myself for the intensity of his tugs. (He might be little but he's *strong!*)

Now, my version of "take" is vastly different from the formal version taught for competition obedience where the dog has to grasp the toy in a specific way. My "take" is an easy, learn-as-you-go type of cue. The next time you're ready to begin a game of tug, formally present the toy to your dog and say "take." Make a show of it—don't just casually toss the toy toward him and say the word. Use two hands and offer the toy to your dog as you say it. If he grabs for the toy before you've said the cue, quickly pull it away before he can latch on or, if you're too late and your dog manages to grab it, drop the toy and walk away. Repeat the process until your dog can wait patiently while you present the toy. Of course, don't forget to praise your dog for doing so!

You don't have to save the "take" cue for the beginning of the game—you can reengage it numerous times during the game. Taking a breather, adjusting your grip on the tug toy, or just testing your dog's ability to listen to cues when he's deep in the game are all excellent opportunities to recycle the cue.

Rule #2: Your dog drops and waits when you ask

"Drop" is the soul of a great game of tug. Without it, chaos reigns. The intensity of the game (read: teeth just inches from your flesh) is easily tempered by this important cue. The good news about teaching "drop" is that you use the same method to teach it for both tug and fetch—if you have a champion fetcher you've probably already planted the seeds for a tug drop.

To get your dog to release something, simply place a treat near his nose when he has the toy in his mouth, and then say "drop" as he opens his mouth to get the treat. If your dog is toy-driven, present an alternate toy as the drop-inducement instead of a treat. Praise your dog for releasing the toy, and then offer it to him again with the "take" cue and resume the game of tug. Practice the drop cue frequently during the game, until your dog understands what the word *drop* means and responds to the cue without needing the treat inducement.

Asking for a drop is a great way to take a break and defuse some of the canine intensity that naturally develops during a spirited round of tug. I let Zeke tug furiously for a few minutes, and then I do a drop/take sequence, which keeps the game unpredictable for him and also tests his ability to focus on me even when he's passionately involved in the game. He tends to go off into a glazed-eye "tug zone" when we play, and the drop/take sequence helps to reel him back to reality.

Warning: Don't shake your dog's head back and forth when you play tug—that can cause injuries. Keep your hand steady and let your dog do the actual tugging.

I taught Zeke the "wait" cue to further test his self-control. The "wait" is another way to keep him from grabbing the toy before I'm ready, but unlike the important game-beginning "take" cue, I employ the "wait" purely as a skill-builder. "Take" is imperative; "wait" is fun. Once we're deep in the game, I'll ask Zeke for a "drop," tell him to "wait," and then slide the toy enticingly on the ground in front of him. He refrains from grabbing it, no matter how I tempt him with it, until I tell him, "Take it!" Impressive!

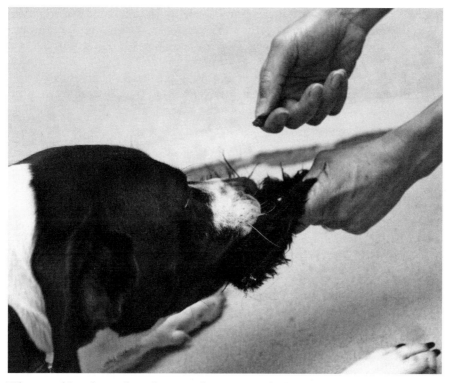

When teaching drop, place the treat close to your dog's nose so that you can deliver the treat and collect the toy almost simultaneously.

"Wait" is yet another easy, train-as-you-go cue. Ask your dog to "drop" and then hold the toy in front of you so that it's mostly contained within your hands. Don't make it difficult on your dog by dangling the toy in front of his nose at this early stage. Simply cup it in your hands and hold it still. Your dog might try to nibble on the exposed ends, but don't let him get to the toy. He'll eventually get bored and back off, and the moment he backs away say, "Wait" in a pleasant voice. (***Remember:*** Your tone of voice counts!) Pause for a second or two, praise your dog quietly for his patience and then tell him, "Take!" If he's unable to resist the toy when you present it and he grabs for it or your hand, drop the toy and walk away. Try again, but offer the toy in a less obvious way on the next attempt. If he couldn't resist the toy when you presented it to him in your hands at his nose level, hold it closer to your body when you offer it instead of reaching it out toward him. Dog teeth on skin is an automatic timeout, so don't allow him to nibble on your hands as you teach the wait cue. Drop the toy and walk away the moment his teeth make contact with your hands.

Don't make your dog wait too long before you tell him to "take" during the early stages of the "wait" training process—a few seconds is a fair starting point. Tell him to "take" and then praise him as he latches on and tugs. Repeat the sequence a few times, presenting the tug toy in a slightly different way each time, exposing more of the toy to your dog each time. (Offer it at nose level, or closer to the ground, or above your dog's head.) As he gets better at waiting, make it tougher on him by slowly moving the toy in front of him. The excitement that builds during the waiting process tests his impulse control, and is an excellent way to temper over-the-top play behavior.

Rule #3: Take frequent training breaks

Still worried about that gateway drug thing? The final rule should quell it for good. Every head-shaking game of tug benefits from a few minutes of training in addition to the many "takes," "waits," and "drops" that are already a part of the process. The bonded dog understands that obedience exercises are a part of everyday life, so it will come as no surprise when you ask your dog to hold a down-stay while you search for a different tug toy, or do a sit-down-sit sequence after a speedy drop.

Taking a training breather allows your dog to cool off and provides you with an easy power shift if you feel as though he's tugging too vigorously. I once worked with a petite woman who wanted to play tug with her Old English Sheepdog (he adored the game) but was put off by her dog's strength. She created a seamless version of tug where the majority of the game was actually training, interspersed with brief periods of tugging. She would ask her dog to hold a stay while she crossed the yard, and then do a "here" and offer the tug toy as the reward. When her dog started pulling the toy with more intensity than she could handle, she'd ask for a "drop" and then begin the process again using a different obedience cue. The benefit was twofold: Her dog was able to safely engage in a beloved activity, and the woman could brush up on their training skills while staying out of the chiropractor's office!

Evasive Maneuvers

This little game is actually training disguised as fun (which, of course, is how all of your dog's training should be!). Evasive Maneuvers is an outdoor game that shows your dog that you are unpredictable—"slippery," if you will—and fun to be near. The trickle-down training benefit is that your dog will be more inclined to keep an eye on you when he's off leash in the park and even while taking leash walks with you throughout the neighborhood. Once again, this game drives home the point that you are unpredictable and *interesting*.

My client Jack lived next to an enormous fenced school field. Dogs weren't allowed on the field during the school year, but the township permitted them during the summer months as long as no stinky evidence was left behind. Jack and his Doberman, Stella, took advantage of the field nearly every day. We visited it during one of our training sessions.

"What do you do with Stella when you're here?" I asked Jack.

"Oh, we usually play fetch and just walk around. She tends to do her own thing when we come here," he laughed.

"Let's switch it up then. I want to teach Stella a silly little game that will help her tune into you more when you hang out at the park. Check this out."

I waited for Stella to glance in my direction (which, thankfully, only took a few seconds), and the moment she did so, I turned my back and walked away from her. Our previous lessons had made it clear to Stella that it was a good idea to keep me in her sights, what with the treats, toys, and general unpredictability I represented, so she stopped examining the grass and took off running in my direction. She caught up to me quickly, and the moment she was close to my side, I gave her a small treat and then turned abruptly in the opposite direction, quickly walking away from her. She caught up to me, and once again I gave her a treat and moved away from her. Stella stood and watched me for a moment before taking off after me, as if she were trying to understand why I kept trying to get away from her. Each time she caught up, I gave her warm praise and a treat, and then turned in a new direction and walked away. From a distance, I'm sure it seemed as though I was desperately trying to get away from the giant Doberman at my side. Each time she fell into step with me, I abruptly walked away from her. Within moments, I couldn't keep her from my side——she was my shadow, nearly impossible to "lose." We looked like we were dancing across the field together.

"Pretty cool, huh?" I shouted to Jack. "Your turn!"

I led Stella over to him and explained the concept of the game. "You're trying to evade her, which seems totally counterintuitive at first. It'll feel weird to move away from him when he catches up to you, but remember: Dogs love to go after rapidly retreating objects! The treats are little reinforcers for checking in with you—they help sweeten the pot. The more creative you can be when you're trying to ditch her, the better. You want her to have to *work* to keep up with you!"

Jack got the message. He turned on his heel and speed-walked away from me as I was finishing up my overview of the game. Stella looked at me, then at Jack, and took off after him. She caught up to him and he rewarded her with a treat. He allowed her to walk beside him for a few steps, praising her

Illegal hold

Jumping up on you during Evasive Maneuvers is an automatic timeout. The game can get spirited, but your dog must keep all four paws on the ground while you play. If he jumps up on you, stop walking, turn your back to him, and stand still for a few seconds. This abrupt withdrawal of your attention should be enough to signal that he crossed the line. When you resume, walk at a slower pace. If the jumping continues, end the game for the day.

for staying close. "Nice improv!" I shouted to him. I watched him praise her once more, then stop dead in his tracks and turn and walk in the opposite direction. Stella caught up to him quickly. Jack tossed her another treat, this time jogging away from her. It lit a fire beneath her, and from that point on the two of them ran in a parallel zigzags across the field as if connected by an invisible thread. Stella was now Jack's shadow.

The three of us visited the field the following week, and I could see the change in Stella. My fun little throw-away Evasive Maneuvers game had changed her. She still ran to the corners of the field when we arrived, and happily dashed after the ball when Jack tossed it, but she kept an eye on him the entire time. Jack had been using a sneak attack approach with the game, so Stella never knew when it was to begin. Sometimes he tossed the ball for her a few times, and then walked away after the third throw. Stella knew that when Jack moved away from her, the game was on. Sometimes he'd surprise her when she caught up, and instead of giving her a treat he'd whip out a tug hidden in his pocket and engage her that way. He was so unpredictable and fun about the game that Stella couldn't help but be captivated by him.

And I was captivated by Jack's creativity. He had taken the game and seamlessly incorporated it into their daily routine, adding his own improvisations to keep Stella guessing. He found an excellent way to help Stella to focus on him in a distracting environment—and have fun while doing it!

Refugee from cat-land

Sumner didn't know how to play when we brought him home. Groomed to be a show dog for the first year of his life, the concept of fun for fun's sake was lost on him. Zeke couldn't figure out why his new sibling refused to latch onto the tug toy when he presented it, or why he didn't run after the ball when I tossed it. We both felt handicapped by Sumner's play deficiency.

I tapped into Sumner's innate but bottled love of play accidentally one afternoon on a deserted soccer field. Zeke was dashing around off leash, but because Sumner was new to me, I opted to keep him on a long line. He had 20 feet of leash and could run a decent distance when I threw the ball for Zeke, but he chose not to. He was unmoved by Zeke's zeal for fetch. I was desperate to chip through his reserve—the guy was *boring!* Plus, I knew that our many walks weren't putting a dent in his young-dog energy levels. I noticed a fluorescent orange corner flag on a six-foot fiberglass pole lying on the ground and picked it up. Sumner was immediately intrigued by the flutter. I held it out to him and he moved toward it. I then dropped the plastic flag part to the ground, slid it back and forth it in front of him, and—bingo!—a game star was born! Sumner took off after the flag like it was alive. He was transfixed by it, and soon Zeke joined him in the chase. Sumner was so focused on the flag's movement that I was able to safely drop his leash and allow him to track the flag all over the field. The long fiberglass pole enabled me to make the flag dance unpredictably, so Sumner never knew which

Sumner chasing the very flag pole that kick-started his love of play.

direction to run. Sometimes I skidded it along the ground, sometimes I bounced it into the air—the unpredictability was part of the fun.

Eight years later, I still occasionally break out the flag pole, but his love of chase inspired me to create more dog-friendly versions of the toy. I created a rubber chase toy—a latex toy on flexible rubber plumber's tubing—and a plush version on a five-foot elastic cord that I call the Flat Cat. Although it's obvious that cats enjoy chasing toys on a string, it's not common knowledge that dogs enjoy that type of play as well. But it makes sense: Dogs love to dart after squirrels, so why wouldn't they also like to chase after a scurrying, life-like fuzzy thing? I've found that my dog version of the quintessential cat toy can coax my play-aversive canine clients to get in the game. Few dogs can resist a rapidly retreating object!

Flat Cat etymology

The name I selected for my toy, Flat Cat, sounds ominous, but the toy was actually named for the creatures that inspired *Star Trek*'s Tribbles, from Robert A. Heinlein's 1952 science-fiction novel, *The Rolling Stones*. His Flat Cats were small, furry, featureless creatures that purred. Mine is a small, furry, featureless creature that squeaks.

The rules for toy on a string play are simple: he should be able to "take" and "drop" when you ask, just like tug, and the toy should always remain on the ground as it races around the room. Dangling the toy in the air encourages jumping. I strive to teach the "four paws on the floor" concept to every dog I meet, and I don't want a constructive game to accidentally lead to inappropriate behavior. Toy on a string is my "secret weapon game" that never fails to surprise dog owners ("Who knew my dog enjoyed playing like a cat?") and enchant dogs.

The Brain Games

Find the Toy

Stuck in the middle of a monsoon and your dog's climbing the walls because he can't get outside to romp? Tired of playing fetch in the hallway? Welcome to my all-time favorite inclement-weather brain game! Find the Toy is my go-to game when hard-core outdoor play isn't an option because of weather or injury, or when nothing seems to put a dent in a dog's energy level. The beauty of the game is that it taps into one of your dog's most amazing but overlooked natural talents. When you play with your dog, you always engage sight, sound, touch, and taste, but what about the forgotten sense, smell? I've found that a few rounds of Find the Toy exhausts a dog almost as effectively as a rousing game of fetch.

Find the Toy is like search and rescue, minus the distressing missing-person element. The concept is deceptively simple: You hide a toy and then encourage your dog to find it using just his sense of smell. Though the description doesn't make it sound exciting, I can't say enough about this amazing game. I play it with Zeke and Sumner both inside the house and out, and it never fails to leave them panting after just two rounds! They've gotten so good at it that I can hide the toy a few feet up off the ground in tree branches or up on a shelf and they *still* manage to find it. I love to watch them tap into their scenting abilities. Each time I hide the toy, I'm sure I've stumped them, only to have them uncover it within minutes. My toy hiding abilities are in a constant battle with their impressive toy *finding* abilities!

It's fascinating to watch dogs scenting, particularly when you know what they're looking for and where it is. Sometimes the dog will zero in on the toy immediately, as if he saw where you put it. Other attempts will illustrate how elusive a scent can be. I've seen dogs literally walk on *top* of the toy several times before finding it, or look at it without registering that it's there. The snuffling, air tasting, and near-misses are all a part of the fun. And those are the very aspects that will tax your dog's brain!

The biggest challenge of the game is selecting a toy your dog deigns worthy of finding. Try using a toy that's either brand new (taking your dog's toy preferences into account—don't use a latex toy if your dog prefers stuffed goods) or that has been out of circulation for a while. The toy doesn't have to

Most dogs can't resist this mouse, which is more like a cat toy.

be large. In fact, I've found that smaller toys work better because they're easier to hide. Smallish, fuzzy, squeaky toys or beloved balls are excellent options. I use a four-inch furry squeaky mouse—essentially a cat toy—to teach the game to the uninitiated because the combination of the realistic fur and high-pitched sound make it irresistible to nearly every dog. Though the toy is delicate and can be eviscerated by even the smallest canine mouth, it's still a viable option for the Find the Toy because the thrill of the game revolves around the seeking, not the actual "find." Play with the toy once it's discovered should be short and supervised. It's merely a way to build anticipation for the next round!

The first step to teaching the game is easy and, sadly, unimpressive. The fireworks don't come until your dog understands how to play, but trust me, they *will* come! If your dog's "stay" cue is strong, place him in a down-stay, walk a few steps away and hide the toy so that he sees where you put it. Easy initial hiding spots are under the couch, next to a coffee table, or peeking out from behind an open door. When the toy is in place, turn toward him and tell him "Find it!" Now, he won't know what "Find it" means, but the combination of his excitement over the new toy just a few feet away and your tone of voice will make it clear that he's supposed to get up and grab it. When he does, have a little celebration. Praise him for "finding" the toy, and engage in some low-level tug with it. Ask for a "drop," toss the toy for him, and then when he brings it back, ask him to do another drop and reclaim ownership. Repeat this initial "Find it" step several times, so that he makes the

Victoria's top ten indoor toy hiding spots

1. In shoes
2. Under his dog bed
3. On low shelves
4. In empty boxes headed for the trash
5. In between cabinets
6. Behind pillows
7. Tied to door knobs
8. In closets with the door almost shut
9. Resting on the slats underneath kitchen chairs
10. Under the edge of an area rug

connection between the cue "find it," and the idea that he's to seek out the toy. Hide it in a variety of easy, ground-level spots. (Be creative——there's more to your living room than —the couch!)

Once you're confident that he understands the "find it" cue (when he's able to ferret out the toy every time you hide it), it's time to unleash the fireworks. Take him to a different room, ask him to "stay" (or have a helper hold him if his stay isn't up to par) and hide the toy in a spot you've used before, but don't let him see where you put it. Tell him to "find it," and then stand back and let his astounding scenting prowess unfold! Resist the temptation to lead him to the object the first time he has to find the toy "blind." Stand close to the spot if you feel as though he needs some guidance, but don't show him where the toy is hidden. I'll surreptitiously squeak the toy if a newbie dog is way off course, but that's the extent of my hinting. The first blind toy discovery deserves a major praise, but it's usually such an impressive feat that you won't be able to hold back!

My former client Lydia was having a difficult time keeping her active young Toy Poodle, Cora, from running around during her convalescence after a leg-breaking tumble. Cora's youthful spirit made the veterinarian's mandate to take it easy for the first three weeks nearly impossible. Lydia contacted me, desperate for advice about how to burn through Cora's seemingly limitless energy.

"She hasn't destroyed anything in the house in *months,* but now she's so bored that she's chewing the coffee table again! Our slow walk around the block barely puts a dent in her spazzyness. She's going nuts from not being able to run and play, and I don't know what to do! I don't want her to reinjure herself, but we can't go on like this doing nothing but short walks."

"I think I have a solution for you," I told Lydia.

This dog found his toy hidden beneath the couch, but he can't quite reach it.

Cora was an incredibly toy-motivated pup when we worked on her basic obedience training, so I knew that she'd take to Find the Toy quickly. I walked Lydia and Cora through the steps, and it took only three repetitions before Cora had figured out the game. Cora's panting after the short introduction gave Lydia hope that she had found a new way to tire out her injured puppy.

Lydia got in touch with me a week later. "That Find the Toy game is a *lifesaver!*" she raved. "Cora loves it, and it really does wear her out. We play all over the house; the family room, my bedroom, the kitchen, the laundry room, and even the master bath! I can't believe that she can find it every single time—that nose of hers is amazing. The best part is that we play for fifteen minutes or so and she's so tired that she stops to take a break. She usually *never* stops playing!"

I suggested that Lydia continue to change up the game, incorporating new toys, and when Cora was up to it, playing it in the backyard.

Moving the game outside adds a new level of difficulty and fun. Your dog has to filter through the millions of intriguing scents around him ("Was that *eau de chipmunk* on the fence?") and zero in on the hidden toy. It's helpful to begin the outdoor version of the game the same way you began the indoor version: Let him watch you hide the toy for the first few cycles. Outside Hide the Toy burns through even more energy because the inherent scent competition, as well as the larger playing field. I was wary the very first time I moved the Find the Toy game from inside my house to the backyard. (I made it extra tough on my dogs and didn't allow them to see me hide the

Victoria's top ten (or so) outdoor toy hiding spots

1. In the wood pile
2. Under shrubbery
3. Under deck furniture
4. Beneath the overhang of large rocks
5. In low-hanging tree branches
6. In loose grass clippings
7. Flush with the fence line
8. On the garden gate trim
9. In potted plants
10. Nestled in the climbing vines
11. On top of the garbage can
12. Hanging from the spigot

first outdoor toy. They were already toy-finding pros by the time we moved outdoors.) We have an active squirrel population that keeps Zeke and Sumner busy when they're outside, so I wasn't sure that my lowly squeaky toy would be enough to keep them focused on the game. Was I wrong! Though they were momentarily derailed by the size of the new playing field (I could see the, "Are you kidding?" in their expressions), they managed to zero in on the hidden toy jaw-droppingly quickly. Squirrels, neighbors, chipmunks—nothing kept them from the game. No matter where I hid it, from tree branches to under large stones, they found it every time.

Find the Toy is an incredibly fun way to showcase your dog's scenting prowess. It's a unique bond builder that's unlike traditional games because it requires your dog to focus his scenting abilities for sport. The pleasant trickle-down effect of that concentration is that your dog will be mentally taxed after a few rounds!

Find Me

This game is another favorite for both the human and canine members of my household. Find Me is the live-action version of Find the Toy: Instead of hiding an object, a member of the household hides and waits to be found. Even my less-inclined-to-play-games husband can't resist the fun of Find Me. It's yet another way to allow our dogs to showcase their natural tracking abilities—plus, it's a great foundation game for our everyday recall.

Zeke and Sumner usually hear my husband arrive home from work each day and rush to greet him at the door, but on the rare instances they don't, Tom kicks into play mode. He'll call me from his cellphone, voice muffled, and tell me that he's hiding in the house. Game on! I turn to the guys and say, "Find him!" and watch them flip into Bloodhound mode. They tear from room to room, tasting the air as much as sniffing it, trying to pinpoint his location. When they finally find him, often a full five minutes later, the joy (and relief) of the discovery is palpable. Zeke hops up and down and Sumner yodels his happiness. We both swear that they seem proud when they find our hiding spots!

We once tested the strength of their tracking abilities after I returned home from a long weekend away. I gave Tom a big hug to plant my scent and then sent him into the house alone. I went around to the backyard and ducked behind a low retaining wall, expecting that they might eventually pick up on my scent when they went outside to potty. Not a chance. Tom told them to "Find her!" and then let them out. Both dogs rushed directly to my hiding spot without even pausing. I was impressed—they aced an extreme version of the game!

This game is similar to a hide-and-seek recall, where you dash around a corner and call your dog to you using your recall word. The difference is that, when you do a recall with your dog, it's a good idea to make kissy noises or whistle to help your dog to find you. In Find Me, your dog must use only his sense of smell to discover your location. It's another variation of the search-and-rescue concept without the rescue aspect.

Much like Find the Toy, Find Me is simple to teach and rather unimpressive at first. The setup is the same: Ask your dog to hold a stay (or have a helper hold him) and hide in an obvious spot, like around the corner from your dog. Say, "Find me!" in a happy tone of voice, and then wait. When he comes around the corner and discovers you, give him big-time praise. Repeat the process, hiding in different easy locations, until your dog is readily seeking you out. I'll occasionally bend the rules if a dog is having a difficult time during the initial stages and make little noise to help him along. This game calls for creativity once your dog figures it out—it won't be much fun for either of you if you only hide around corners or in closets. Feeling agile? Try hiding on top of the washing machine!

I incorporate this game into my everyday life frequently. I flit around my house constantly, so my dogs no longer follow me every time I leave the room, but they do tend to check up on me if I'm out of sight or silent for more than a few minutes. To keep life unpredictable for them, I'll often duck behind a door and say the magic phrase, "Find me!" It's amazing how quickly Zeke and Sumner turn from slumbering blobs to heat-seeking missiles! It's impossible for me to play only one round of the game, so I usually wind up engaging them a few more times before I settle down and get back to business. Find Me is a fun, quick way to burn through some energy and keep life surprising for your pooch!

Find Me is hide-and-seek for dogs!

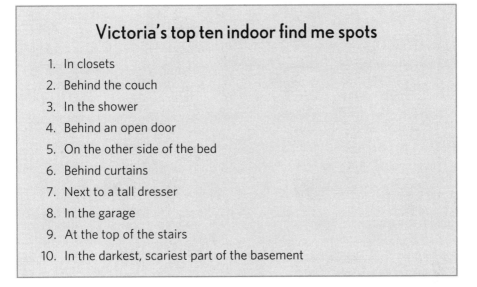

Victoria's top ten indoor find me spots

1. In closets
2. Behind the couch
3. In the shower
4. Behind an open door
5. On the other side of the bed
6. Behind curtains
7. Next to a tall dresser
8. In the garage
9. At the top of the stairs
10. In the darkest, scariest part of the basement

It's Tricky

Trick training opened a new world of training for Zeke and me. That simple "roll over" that had eluded us for so long using traditional training methods was the first step to a rich variety of tricks. Though there's a critical need to teach basic obedience behaviors, both for safety and control, teaching tricks is a fun way to hone your skills as a trainer and add to your dog's vocabulary. There's no pressure when attempting tricks—it's purely fun for fun's sake. And having fun with him is yet another way to deepen your bond.

Every dog should have at least one cute trick up his sleeve. One of my favorites (which just happens to be easy to teach) is "spin." This trick transforms your dog into a twirling top, turning around in circles over and over. I use this trick as a "say please" behavior with my guys when we're about to play, and they get so excited that their spins come out fast and hoppy—and adorable.

The most difficult part to teach is the very first step. The goal is to place the treat close to his nose and move it in a circular motion just above his head, as if you're stirring a large pot. In a perfect world, he follows the treat's path, but what usually happens is he either sits politely or leaps at the treat. To avoid the automatic sit, start the "pot stirring" motion while your dog is moving toward you, rather than trying to begin the behavior while he's already seated. To avoid the leaping, keep the treat very close to his nose so he isn't tempted to jump for it. The circular movement should be steady. Don't whip your hand in a small tight circle and expect him to follow! Give the treat to him right as he reaches "the point of no return," meaning he's completed at least 180 degrees of the circle.

Zeke doing his wave trick. (Or maybe he's getting ready for high five?)

Repeat the pot-stirring motion several times, until he's able to smoothly follow the treat's path. Wait to give him the treat until he's completed the full circle. Now attempt the pot-stirring movement *without* the treat in your hand.

This prevents the "ransom" scenario, where he'll only perform the trick if he knows you have a goody ready to go. Pay up with a treat that was hidden in your pocket after he has completed the full circle.

At this point your pot stirring movement is still big and obvious, but the trick is more impressive if he can respond to a verbal cue and a small hand signal. (Picture stirring a drink with your pointer finger.) With that in mind, each pot-stir movement should get less and less obvious, until you can do a subtle spinning hand signal using just your wrist. At this point, you're ready to add the verbal cue. Say "spin!" right as your dog begins the process—you're essentially teaching him English and "naming" the behavior he's performing. Once your dog has connected the word to the behavior (it takes anywhere from ten to twenty repetitions), ask him to do two spins in a row!

When teaching spin, keep the treat close to your dog's nose and keep the luring movement smooth.

Asking for the spin prior to an activity your dog really loves to do—for example, taking a walk—will encourage a speedier response to the cue. The joy of the pending activity will spill over into the trick he's performing. Spin is a fun little party trick that's easy to teach and adorable to watch!

The painful paw

I'm a fool for dog tricks, but one that I avoid teaching is "paw," unless the dog in question has tremendous self-control. In my world, "paw" or "shake" means that he places his paw in your hand when you ask. Unfortunately, the paw trick tends to turn into, "I'd like your attention so I'm going to rake my paw down your leg repeatedly," or, "You taught me to do something with my paw and I know that you have treats in your pocket so I'm going to throw my paw in your lap over and over until you pay up." Shake is a fine trick, but it should always mean "paw in my hand when I ask" not "paw thrashing wildly."

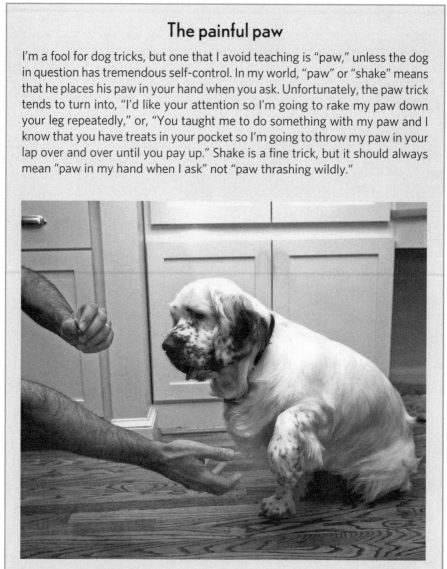

Paw can be a cute trick, but make sure it doesn't turn into an attention-seeking behavior.

Actions speak louder ...

Why don't I suggest adding the verbal cue right away? Dogs pay attention to body language first and spoken language second. If you add the verbal cue when you're still doing an exaggerated pot-stirring motion, that over-exaggerated movement is then "cemented" as part of the cue. Your dog won't recognize your verbal request to "spin" without it. It's best to fine-tune and minimize the body language portion of the trick before you add the verbal cue.

Not All Play Is Constructive

Enthusiastic play is good for your dog, and for your bond. That said, there are a few "games" that are often mistaken for constructive play that should be avoided. Appropriate play can *seem* wild and out of control, but sanctioned dog-safe games always have a set of clear rules that keep play healthy for all parties no matter how vigorous the action gets! The rules keep your dog from lapsing into inappropriate behavior like nipping hands, jumping up, and acting too rough or pushy. The following are a few of the games to avoid because they encourage those very types of responses.

Wrestling

Richard invited me over to help him deal with his Bernese Mountain Dog Toby's intense greeting behavior. I saw it firsthand when I arrived at their house. Toby leapt at me making high-pitched yipping noises. He grabbed at my jacket. "As you can see he's out of control when people come over. Because he's a Berner, the jumping up and mouthiness can be pretty painful."

Once I had righted myself after Toby's welcome, I asked for more detail. "Does he do it to everyone who comes to your house?"

"Yeah, it's a given that if you walk through that front door, you're gonna get tackled."

"So he jumps up on you, too?"

"Oh, yeah, definitely. But he knows that when I get home it's play time!"

"Well, consistent play is a good thing. What do you do with Toby?" I knew what was coming next.

"We wrestle around. I roll on the ground with him—I try to pin him, he tries to pin me. It's pretty intense. I mean, he bites me, but it's usually gentle and it's all in good fun." I could see the light bulb going off as Richard explained the game to me. He knew what I was about to say.

"I hate to break this to you. . . . I love that you're dedicated to playing with Toby, but I'm not in love with the game. His initial interactions with you at the front door are all about getting physical. There's no room for polite behavior if every interaction with you at the door revolves around wrestle mania. His behavior with your guests is just an extension of what you've taught him is an acceptable way to interact."

"I guess that means that letting my poker buddies do the same thing when they come over only makes it worse, right?"

As we sat and chatted, Toby tried to engage me in a round of tug. He brushed his toy up against my hand repeatedly, but I ignored the pushy behavior. Toby escalated to a cheerful but incredibly loud bark at me, then a play bow, and then launched himself into my lap and began thrashing around.

"This is the trickle-down effect of all the wrestling," I said as I removed myself from Toby's grip. "When he wants to engage, he does what he knows works: jumping up, mouthing, and pawing. I'm guessing that this is how he gets your attention when he wants something. Do you wrestle with him when he jumps on you like he just did to me?"

"Unless I'm in the middle of doing something, I usually give in to him. And my friends do it too. We all play rough." I watched as Toby walked over to Richard, nibbled his fingers and got some pats under the chin as his reward.

"Wrestling blurs the lines of acceptable behavior. These rough interactions might be tolerable for you and your college buddies, but what happens when your grandmother comes over for a visit? Or your date who's afraid of dogs?"

"Yeah, Toby *has* scared off a few women," Richard admitted with a grin. "I guess this means no more wrestling, huh?"

"You read my mind. I'm not a big fan of wrestling because it can lead to just this type of unchecked nuttiness. Energetic play is totally fine, but you need to instill some rules. The most important is that you should always have a toy between you and Toby when you play. No more hands-on rough stuff. Does he nip at you if you try to wipe his feet or towel him off?"

"Oh, yeah. Every time I touch him he thinks I want to wrestle. He'll only let me pet him when he's exhausted. Now that I think about it, it *is* a little frustrating. I just never made the connection between the wrestling and everything else he was doing."

I break many male hearts when I tell them that dog-human jujitsu isn't a good idea. Richard was no exception. He loved the interactions with Toby, but he could see that the game had leached into every part of his life with Toby, even petting. To combat their history of rough play, I suggested that Richard introduce a "toy only" rule: Play commences only when there's a toy between the two of them. When Toby grazed his teeth on Richard, he was to mark the infraction with a loud, dramatic "Ouch!" and walk away from Toby. If Toby persisted by jumping up or nipping at his back, Richard was to escalate to leaving the room. Social isolation is a powerful dog-safe punisher, and if Richard's timing was good—meaning the "punishment" of leaving the room came mere seconds after the infraction—Toby would soon catch on that his actions were making his favorite person walk out on him. Richard promised to make his friends obey the new household rules as well. Because Toby had a long rough-play history, it was going to take time and dedication to erase the temptation for both dog and human. I knew that Richard was committed to the cause the next time I showed up at his house: He'd posted a sign near his front door with the new "How to play with Toby" rules!

Slap the Puppy and other hand games

This game usually begins in puppyhood. He nibbles on your hand and you playfully swat him away. He makes that adorable little "I'm a tough guy" face, gives a little growl or bark and comes back at you again. You repeat the swat. This turns into a game of swat/bite, which then morphs into an inappropriate face and muzzle slapping game. Not good. Any game that encourages your dog to bite you is a bad idea. Much like wrestling, this face-slapping game blurs the lines of acceptable play. Plus it's just not nice. Play is supposed to strengthen the bond between you and your dog—hitting him on the face repeatedly certainly won't make that happen. The argument that "Dogs play hard with each other—why can't I?" always surfaces, but dogs also sniff each other's butts. You're not a dog, and your dog knows that.

Any game that encourages your dog to bite people is a bad idea.

Chase

While I'm not 100 percent against chase games, they *can* lead to mixed signals. A well-executed game of "I'm gonna get you!" with a beginning and an end can be a fine way to play with your dog. My concern is with dogs who assume that every time their owners head for them, it's to play a game of "catch me if you can." The most common reason why someone can't play fetch with her dogs is because once the dog assumes control of the toy, he won't bring it back to her. This tends to force the game of chase. The person then dutifully runs after the dog in an attempt to get the ball back (four legs trump two), and he has a grand time controlling the game.

The other more compelling reason why chase should be relegated to a rule-bound game is because you don't want your dog to think that your approach is a signal to run in the opposite direction. Picture this scene: You're at the dog park and you spot a notorious canine rabble-rouser on the way in. Your small dog is just five steps away from you, so you reflexively move toward him with the intent of picking him up and leaving before the inappropriate dog can start causing trouble. A chase-crazy dog will probably view your rapid approach as an invitation to the game, leaving you frustrated and worried about the furry battering ram heading in your direction as you run after him. It's difficult for a dog to switch from play mode and into training mode to do a recall once a wild, boundary-free game like chase begins.

If you have your heart set on playing chase with your dog, turn it into a choreographed game. Begin with a very clear signal (my occasional chase games with Sumner start with, "Three, two, one, *go!*") so that your dog understands that the commencement of the game isn't signaled just by your approach. Exaggerate your movements as you play. I'll hold my hands in the air in "scary monster position" when I'm playing chase. Enforce the rule that holds true for every game: Don't allow him to jump up on you as you play, no matter how exciting the game becomes. When the game is over, signal the end with a phrase like, "All done," and assume your normal posture. Ignore any attempts to continue the game, like running up to you and dashing away. Adding some basic training to the mix will standardize the game as well. Asking your dog to perform an obedience exercise before signaling the beginning of a round drives home the point that chase doesn't just happen. Though chase is a borderline game, a few boundaries are enough to earn it a yellow light.

No pushy pooches

Don't give in to the game of chase over fetch just because your dog demands it. Throw the ball for him, and if he runs away and "asks" for you to chase, simply walk away. If he follows behind you, turn and ask him to do a "drop" or "trade." If he's unable to execute the behavior or turns and runs away again, take a break from the game.

Play It Again, and Again . . .

Creative play is a no-brainer route to building a stronger bond with your dog. It's fun, it's easy, and if you do it right you should get as much enjoyment out of it as your dog! Investing in the games you play with your dog, rather than playing just to fulfill a daily exercise quota, will transform you from "the person who throws the ball" to someone who is intriguing, challenging, and utterly unpredictable. I've watched relationships blossom through play, my own with Sumner included. The beauty of creative play is that bond building is just one of the benefits. Incorporated into your daily routine, it becomes yet another way to reinforce his good behaviors. You don't have to rely on treats alone to say, "nice work" when he performs his everyday training exercises— a quick round of tug can be an effective reward. And, of course, creative play expends your dog's pent up physical *and* mental energy, leaving you with a thoroughly tired and happy pooch!

The right kind of play will exercise you dog's body and *his brain!*

Chapter 9

BUILDING BLOCK #5: TIME FOR THE TRICKY STUFF

f any of the advice I've given so far has seemed odd to you, stop reading now. Some of my bonding suggestions in this chapter are, admittedly, out there. I happen to think that creative dog bonding—magic moments, if you will—turn everyday events into something remarkable. Life with your dog should be enjoyable, even in the face of frustrations such as rampant squirrel addiction, inattentiveness, and an unquenchable drive to sniff. The suggestions in this chapter will help curb some of your relationship challenges by injecting fun. The core concept behind my tricky bond builders is that, as always, you're *interesting*.

The Squirrel Game

When fall rolls around, the phone calls start coming in: "My dog is crazy about squirrels—she nearly yanks my arm off every time she sees one! How can I make it stop?"

Oh, how I wish I could cast a spell to keep dogs from chasing squirrels! The fact is, you can't easily squelch your dog's urge to pursue rapidly retreating objects (that includes everything from chipmunks to birds), but you *can* temper it with a creative, slightly embarrassing game. The idea behind the game is that your dog is allowed to chase occasionally, if you grant her permission and take off *with* her. This little training game is a fantastic way to strengthen the bond with your dog because not only are you allowing her to engage in a normally prohibited and deeply loved behavior, but you're actually doing it *with* her! Suddenly, you're a rule-breaking partner in crime.

Mark called me because his dog Skipper's squirrel pursuits were causing him back pain. "I'm a big guy," he explained, exasperated. "But this dog can pull like an ox when she sees a squirrel! And it's not just the pulling—it's her surprise acceleration when I'm not looking that's killing me."

"I've been there," I told him. "And if you're willing to make a fool out of yourself around the neighborhood for the next few weeks, I think I have a solution for you."

"I'm willing," he said. "I was really close to getting a choke chain for Skip, but my gut tells me that that's not a good idea."

"Trust your gut—a choke wouldn't help. We can talk about some dog-safe no-pull harnesses and collars, too, but let's give my technique a shot first. That way, we'll have a backup if Skipper opts out of the game."

I met up with Mark and Skipper on a beautiful fall day in their tree-filled neighborhood. Skipper was an impressively large Golden Retriever, and I could see how her pulling could be painful and difficult to control. Mark assured me that she was a perfect leash walker during the non-squirrel seasons. The squirrels were out in full force on the day I met with them, so I was glad I had my sneakers on for the lesson—I was going to need them. We started walking and I described how we were about to tackle Skipper's addiction.

"Here's the thing about squirrels: They're not going away, and you're not going to stop Skipper from wanting to chase them. We're going to teach her that if she sits for you when you ask, then we'll allow her to get crazy and chase a squirrel with you. Over time you'll reduce the number of squirrels you chase during a walk, and, eventually, you'll reduce it even more to maybe just one squirrel dash per week—and she'll be fine with that. The knowledge that she can *sometimes* chase squirrels with you should be enough to keep her from going nuts when she sees squirrels on the horizon. You're tuning her into a gambler: Every time she sees a squirrel, she'll wonder, 'Is *this* the squirrel we can chase?'"

"Okay. . . ." I could tell that Mark was a very agreeable person, but deep down he thought I was nuts.

"First, we're going to get some focus from Skipper in the face of the enemy. The next time we see a squirrel, I'm going to ask her to sit for me. I realize that it'll be tough for her to do it, though."

Just as I finished my sentence, a squirrel raced down a tree right in front of us and then paused. Skipper flipped into alert mode and dashed a few steps toward it, pulling me off balance.

"Wow, she *is* strong. Here's a little trick that'll help. Stand on the leash right at the midpoint so that you can use your full body weight as a brace." I demonstrated the technique.

Harness the energy

A choke chain coupled with rampant pulling can injure a dog's neck and back. A safer, dog-friendly alternative for dogs who strain at the end of the leash is a no-pull harness. A no-pull harness is different from a standard dog harness because, as the name implies, its construction decreases a dog's ability to pull. Though a regular harness won't necessarily decrease pulling, it *is* gentler than a choke collar.

Standing on the midpoint of the leash gives you more control if your dog is pulling toward something.

"Ready? Here comes the sit." I turned toward Skipper and asked her to sit for me, but my voice was as effective as the wind in her fur. She was deep in the primal zone. "We're too close and she can't focus on me, so let's back up a bit." I took a few steps away from the squirrel with Skipper, and then asked for the sit again. She managed to break her stare for a second and look up at my face, so I praised her for the shift in focus.

In the squirrel game, sit comes before the chase.

"This is one exercise where I resort to bribes," I told Mark. "It's not good in your everyday life, but it's fine in this scenario while we help Skipper figure out the rules in an incredibly distracting environment." I took a treat and placed it right in front of Skipper's nose. "Sit," I asked again. We were far enough away from her quarry for her to execute the sit with a cheese inducement. The moment her bum hit the ground, I said, "Let's go!" and took off running with her toward the squirrel in the tree. We didn't come close to catching it, but the thrill of the chase was written all over Skipper's face.

"Wow, I guess I'm going to get into really good shape with all this running," Mark said, looking dubious.

"You missed an important part of my explanation," I said, laughing and panting. "This is just the initial phase of the training. Yes, you're going to be doing some running in the beginning, but not for life. You're going to teach her that you won't chase every single squirrel you encounter during a walk. But I'm getting ahead of myself. You're up next for this first baby step."

It didn't take long before we saw another squirrel. Mark managed to get a speedier sit out of Skipper than I did, and the two of them had a grand time running toward the squirrel. They repeated the process a few times, and Skipper managed to sit a little faster with each attempt.

"Now that Skipper is starting to catch on that a squirrel in her crosshairs means that a request to sit will follow, we're going to make it tougher on her. Not only does she need to sit, but she needs to hold it for a few seconds before we'll begin the chase. The next time you see a squirrel, get her to sit, and then praise her quietly for a few moments. This step instills a little patience, so her sit doesn't turn into a bum-then-run routine. This isn't a formal stay—I'm only looking for maybe three seconds initially." Mark tried it the next time he saw a squirrel and, surprisingly, Skipper managed to hold her sit until he said, "Let's go!"

"I hate to be rude—this is fun and all—but why am *I* chasing squirrels with her? Isn't that encouraging the behavior?" Mark asked.

"That's not rude at all—I told you that this is a weird way of dealing with the issue. We're basically trying to shift the balance of power during your walks, though I hate using the word *power*. Right now, if Skipper sees squirrels, she has the option to chase whether you want her to or not. She just takes off and jerks you along for the ride. Asking her to sit and wait is a subtle way of telling Skipper that you're on the leash, too, and you have a say about what happens during the walk. If she can focus on you and execute a sit in the face of such a major-league distraction, you'll reward her with the thing she wants more than anything: to run freely after her prey. Adding the few seconds of hold time helps to underscore the idea that self-control leads to good things. That self-control should have a trickle-down effect during your walks, too. Instead of going out of her head every time she spots a squirrel, she'll look to you for direction to find out if the squirrel before you is indeed chaseable."

A speedy, attentive sit is rewarded with a chance to chase the squirrel.

I continued, "You're going to do this sit-for-a-squirrel thing for the next few days at least. If you're dedicated and you don't mind your neighbors staring out their windows at you, a full week or two would be lovely. Play with how long you make her sit before you chase—sometimes only wait a second, other times make her hold that sit for five seconds before you take off. Now here's the secret sauce: You're also going to teach her that you have the ability, as holder of the leash, to ignore some of the squirrels you encounter. If she sets her sights on a squirrel across a busy road, simply tell her, 'Not today,' and give her a treat. You'll be met by shock the first time you turn down the chance to chase, but that preemptive reward should ease the pain of not chasing. And don't forget to praise her like crazy after you give her that treat. You want to shift her focus to *you,* not the squirrel. In time, *not today* will be conditioned to mean, 'Come get paid.'"

"But how will she know what *not today* means?" Mark asked. "Do I have to teach her?"

"I break all sorts of dog-training rules, and this is an example of yet another one. I consider it a learn-as-you-go kind of cue. Your body language, your tone, and the treat will all help her understand that *not today* means, 'Keep moving with me.'"

We walked on and didn't see any squirrels for a block, and then we heard a commotion high in the trees above us. Squirrel fight!

"Not today!" Mark said cheerfully, offering Skipper a treat. Perhaps she knew that the squirrels were out of her reach, or maybe she was just brilliant, but Skipper moved along without a complaint.

"I'm impressed!" I said, "It's actually a little early in the process to begin the not-today step, but you both nailed it."

"Yeah, I knew it was risky, but I figured that since the squirrels weren't really chaseable, I'd give it a shot," Mark said. "Usually that kind of commotion above her would make her stop in her tracks and stare up. I'm surprised she was able to keep going."

We continued chatting as we walked, and our attention strayed from Skipper. Unfortunately, she spotted a rogue squirrel on the ground before we did and took off. Mark did his best not to be dragged along behind her.

"Guess we're back at square one, huh?" Mark asked, rubbing his shoulder as he walked back to me.

"That's the drawback to this technique—it isn't failsafe. Dogs have a leg up when it comes to spotting squirrels, so they'll lock on to ones that you don't even see. It's also not appropriate for everyone. A woman with a baby carriage or a senior dog owner wouldn't be able to execute it. In those cases, a no-pull harness is a great first step, along with some clicker training. I think a harness would be helpful for you and Skipper, too, to avoid situations just like this. You should still continue working toward a not-today way of life using the technique we just did. She'll be able to pull after squirrels a little, even with a no-pull harness on, but she won't able to do it as forcefully. That'll save your back. Now, we can do the clicker approach if you want and skip this madness completely."

"No, I like this approach," Mark said. "I can see how it'll work for her. So for the next week or so, I'm going to get Skipper to sit every time we see a squirrel."

"Every time you see an *accessible* squirrel," I reminded him. "Don't bother with the ones across the street or in the middle of your least favorite neighbor's yard. You'll still get a reaction from her for those initially, but the no-pull harness will help."

"Right. So every time we see a squirrel that's within range I get her to sit for me, pause for a few seconds, and then we take off toward the squirrel."

"Exactly."

"Then, after about a week of chasing, I'm going to introduce the not-today concept, where she'll see a squirrel and I'll say 'Not today,' give her a treat, and keep walking."

"Right, but you're not going to blow off every squirrel you see. Just some of them, and you'll continue to chase other ones."

Worth watching

Training a watch cue is a helpful alternative if chasing squirrels isn't an option for you—it's a way to get your dog to focus on you instead of furry distractions (including cats, chipmunks, and other dogs). Start practicing this behavior in your home before you put it to work in squirrel land.

To teach it, place a tasty treat in front of your dog's nose, and then draw the treat up to your face. Hold the treat next to your eyes, and then click and treat to mark the moment her gaze meets yours. Repeat the process a few times, click-treating each time she looks up to your face, and then turn away from her—she'll probably come around to your front to see your face again. Right as she glances up, say "Watch!" and then click and treat. Repeat the process without the luring movement and continue to name the behavior (say "Watch!" as she looks up).

Eventually you should be able to say "Watch!" and your dog will look up toward your face. Practice it in a variety of situations so that the behavior becomes fluent. Increase the duration of her gaze before you deliver the treat by praising her quietly as she looks at your face.

Once she's consistently gazing up at your face when you say "Watch!", you can attempt it outside during a walk. Ask her to watch as you stroll along, praise her for holding your gaze for a few steps, and then deliver the treat. When you've perfected the watch, ask for it just before she locks onto a squirrel in your path, and get her to hold your gaze until the squirrel darts up a tree!

"Yeah. And over time I'll opt out of chasing more squirrels, until we can pass by most of them without her freaking out."

"That's it. I know it sounds weird, but it works! I did it with my two dogs and now we'll go months without chasing one. They know that I make the call about chasing, even when one runs right in front of us. They tense up, but unless I ask for the sit and then say, 'Let's go!', they keep walking."

"Fingers crossed!" Mark said with a grin.

The squirrel game is an unusual but powerful approach to dealing with a squirrel-fixated dog. It works because it requires your dog to ask permission to engage in a formerly forbidden pleasure, and then taps into the innate gambler in every dog by not allowing her to chase every squirrel she encounters. She has to look to you, the holder of the leash, to make the call about the chase, which reinforces the idea that you play a role in the pursuit, too. You're a participant. Instead of fighting against a genetically programmed behavior, you're harnessing it.

Amazing Discoveries

I'll admit it: This bond-building suggestion is the strangest.

I grew up used to scanning the ground looking for wildflowers, morels, salamanders, frogs, turtles, and deer tracks. It's a habit that continues to this day (thanks, Dad), and because of it, I often find things during our walks that my dogs missed. It all started with a chipmunk hole during a springtime walk years ago. Zeke and Sumner were looking in a different direction when a chipmunk dashed right in front of us and down into his camouflaged hole.

"How did they miss that?" I wondered.

"Zeke, Sum, come check this out!" I kneeled down and pointed to the hole, which I was sure was coated with fresh chipmunk scent. They hunkered down shoulder to shoulder, put their noses flush with the hole, and breathed it in. Snort, sniff, huff, puff. Their excited reactions spurred me on.

"Where's the chippie?" I asked. I pointed back to the hole. "He's in there, guys! Get him!"

Sumner raked his big Boxer paw at the hole and snuffed at it again. I knew that the chipmunk was safely below, but the thrill of the fresh scent made it seem temptingly near.

Their gleeful reactions convinced me to become another pair of eyes for my dogs. A bonded dog believes that her person is pretty darn interesting, and amazing discoveries help to drive that point home. It's essentially teaching your dog that sticking close to you is a good idea, because you uncover fascinating treasures that she passed right by.

Any time I find something that I think would be of interest to my dogs, I point it out. Like what? Here are some of our favorites:

- A squished frog in the street
- The water drain where we spotted a cat, years ago

- Feathers
- Fallen bird nests
- Cracked bird eggs that have fallen from the nest
- Nooks in trees that probably once housed animals
- Roadkill (just a quick sniff from a distance)
- Holes in the ground
- Animal tracks
- Shed deer antlers
- Abandoned items on the street, like sunglasses, hair clips, and toys
- Fur hanging on low branches

Your dog might take her investigation too far and grab the items you're pointing out to her. Use your well-honed drop cue to get her to release the goods.

My parents live on a lovely wooded property that's the crossroads to many different wild animals. When we visit them, we have ample opportunity to put the amazing discoveries bond-builder to work. For example, the resident deer bed in the same area of the woods each night, so I make sure to walk the dogs toward the matted-down grass that the deer leave behind in the morning. I take them to the edge of the pond to show them the hundreds of frogs sunning themselves. I point out the raccoon tracks in the mud. As soon as they hear me say, "Hey, guys, check this out!", they know that I've stumbled upon something worthy of notice.

The amazing-discoveries technique requires you to think like a dog and occasionally get your hands dirty in the name of bond building. Whenever I suggest it to my clients, they give me a look that says, "Really?" to which I reply, "Yes, *really*. It works."

My clients Jim and Anna wanted to work on their dog Munson's trail-walking skills. They excelled with their basic obedience lessons, but Munson tended to lose his head when they hit the trail. The new scents and uncharted terrain overwhelmed him. We decided to meet at a local park for their final session to address the issue at the source. I arrived at the park early and planted a variety of intriguing items along the path we were about to walk. I even went so far as to tie little ribbons to the branches above the hidden surprises, just to make sure I didn't accidentally pass by any of them. I didn't tell Jim and Anna about the treasure hunt as we set off—I merely "stumbled upon" the first item, a clump of Samoyed fur I'd gotten from another client's dog brush and tangled in the low branches.

"Check this out, cutie! What's this?"

Munson rushed over to where I was kneeling and breathed in the fur's scent.

"I wonder who was here?" I winked at Jim and Anna and continued walking. A short distance later we came to my next sting, an abandoned bird's nest I'd found in my backyard.

Take time to smell the birds' nests.

"Hey, Muns," I called. "What is *this?*"

He trotted back to me and buried his nose in the nest, taking special interest in the feathers clinging to the edge.

By this time, Anna had spotted the ribbons. "You did this?" she asked me, pointing at a ribbon.

"I did! We agree that Munson's issue when he's in the woods is that he finds everything else much more interesting than you and Jim. This little game will help shift his focus back to you, when used in combination with proper loose-leash walking techniques. I'm not saying that you have to walk the trail and plant stuff prior to coming out, of course. Just keep your eyes open and point out cool stuff to him every now and then. It's actually really fun. And you don't have to wait to do it on the trails—do it anytime you see something weird or interesting when you walk around the neighborhood. Remember, we want him to think that you bring the fun."

We continued walking. Suddenly, I heard Anna call out, "Munsie! What's *this?*"

He sped to her side and investigated the kicked-up patch of soil she was pointing out. She looked over her shoulder at me and said, "It looks like something was scratching around here."

Munson ran his nose over the freshly turned up earth and began digging at it.

"Looks like you're right!" I said.

Jim joined in on the game as we continued the walk, and, by the end, Munson was walking closer to us, eager to zoom in on our next discovery. We took care to point out only worthy curiosities on the trail so as not to overdo the game. The combination of their skill with the loose-leash walking techniques coupled with the occasional amazing discovery was enough to help Munson keep from pulling wildly down the path.

Amazing discoveries alone won't reform a confirmed leash puller, but this technique *will* help to put a dent in the behavior. It's strange, it's fun, and it works!

Get Lost

There's a lot going on at the average dog park. Bums to sniff, balls to chase, people to jump on—it's no wonder your dog has a hard time checking in with you. The other side of the equation is that you probably follow the same script every time you visit the dog park. You plant yourself next to the crowd of dog people and chat the time away, rarely moving from your station until it's time to leave. And your dog depends on that fact. There's no need to check in with you because she knows exactly where you are and exactly what you're doing.

My first piece of advice for every dog-parking dog owner is to become "slippery": Move around the park constantly, so your dog learns to keep one eye on the game and one eye on you. It's a deceptively simple way to get her to remember that you came to the park *with* her, and that you're more than just a chauffeur and door opener.

Ollie's people, Davis and Eileen, loved taking him to play at the dog park. He was a high-energy American Eskimo/Boston Terrier mix who benefited greatly from twice-weekly trips to play with his canine buddies. The problem was that he took off like a shot the moment they arrived and never gave them a glance until they called him (repeatedly) to leave. Ollie was so eager to play that he often did so to the detriment of his own health—his short muzzle left him gasping for air. Davis and Eileen were looking for a way to get Ollie to occasionally stop playing during their visits and take quick catch-your-breath breaks with them before going back to play. Ollie's recall was decent, but short of leashing him up or grabbing him, it was impossible to get him to slow down for more than a drive-by, "Hi! Bye!"

"We're going to use a two-step approach," I told them, as we walked to their local dog park on an early weekday morning. "I picked a non-rush-hour time to meet because we want to polish up his skills when the park is less distracting. Let's stack the deck in our favor."

There were only five other dogs when we arrived. "Just do what you normally do when you get to the park," I advised. Davis unclipped Ollie's leash and we watched the contrail of dirt form behind him as he rushed to greet his friends.

"And that's the last we'll see of him until it's time to go," Davis said.

"What do you guys do while he's off playing?"

"A lot of our friends come here, so we chat and drink coffee. We usually hang out by the picnic table," Eileen said.

"Uh-oh, your friends aren't going to like me very much. We're going to switch things up from now on. See, Ollie is used to coming to the park and having you two cemented here by the bench. You're predictable and—excuse me for saying this—a little boring. But not anymore."

"We'd play fetch with him and be more exciting that way, but he doesn't want to play with the ball when we're here," Eileen said. "All he wants to do is chase and wrestle."

"And that's understandable," I told her. "This is his time to hang out with his friends, and I'm not suggesting that you deny him that opportunity and make him focus completely on you. Now *that* would be boring, and it would negate the reason for coming in the first place! Initially, all I want him to do is come over and check in with you occasionally. How do we accomplish that? We move."

With that, I began walking toward the other end of the park with Davis and Eileen in tow. "I want Ollie to realize that you two are hard to keep track of. You're no longer the same old predictable people who hang out in one spot the whole time you're here. You move around *constantly*. It might take him a while to catch on, but the good news is that this game isn't hard to play. It's also a little devious. I want Ollie to have an 'Oh no!' moment. I want him to glance toward where you normally stand, realize that you're not there, and get a little worried about where the heck you've gone."

Eileen chuckled. "Wouldn't that be nice? Ollie, worried about *us* for a change?"

We stood in our new position for a few minutes, watching Ollie rumble with an agreeable Lab mix and a wiry Boxer. Ollie took a turn at the bottom of the scrum and then emerged and shook his body off in a way that signaled more than his desire to remove debris from his fur. He was overwhelmed and wanted to have a chance on top of the pile. The Lab and Boxer continued rolling and biting without Ollie. He glanced to where Davis and Eileen normally stood and froze.

"Did you see that? Awesome! He noticed that you're not there!" I crowed. We stood near the fence at the far edge of the dog park.

Ollie moved away from the dogs, swinging his head from left to right, scanning the people in the park. He walked to the group of people congregated at the picnic table and kept moving when he realized that his eyes hadn't deceived him and that Davis and Eileen truly weren't among them.

"This is good, this is very good," I said. "He cares that you're missing! He's trying to find you. Now when he finally spots you, praise him. He doesn't have to come all the way up to you at first. Right now, all I want him to do is seek you out and lock onto you."

I hadn't even finished my sentence before Davis crowed, "Good Ollie! You found us! Good boy!" Ollie had, indeed, made his way over to us as I talked. He high-stepped in front of us, basking in his victory.

"Now we're going to 'release' him to go play. He's off leash, so he could release himself just by taking off again, but we're tapping into the idea that you have some control over his actions, leashed or unleashed." I looked down at Ollie and smiled, "Good job, bud! Go play!" I jogged ahead a few steps and Ollie took off toward the growing dog pile in the middle of the park.

"Now we move again. He checked in, so it's time to relocate. Let's see how long it takes him to check in this time."

We walked to the opposite side of the park. Ollie picked his head up from the pack as we passed, and Eileen praised him warmly for it. We continued and found a shady spot under the lone tree.

"If this park had more trees, we could really get crazy," I said. "Hiding behind trees adds another fun wrinkle to the game. But moving from one side of the park to the other is enough to keep him guessing."

Ollie played with the other dogs for a full five minutes and never raised his head. "Is that bad?" Eileen asked. "Shouldn't he check in sooner?"

"Nope, not at this point," I said. "We just started the game—looking for you is a new concept. He's lost in dog-land right now, and that's totally fine. Soon enough, he'll realize that you're not where you left him, and he'll hunt for you again. It'll happen."

A few more minutes passed before Ollie removed himself from the mob. He scanned the park, pacing.

"He looks a little worried," Davis said.

"He probably is, and that's okay. We want him to realize that he needs to keep an eye on you in order to avoid the worry."

Ollie spotted us and his ears perked up. He raced to our new hiding spot as the three of us praised him like a gospel choir.

"Now it's time for part two of the game. You mentioned that one of the reasons you want him to come to you more frequently at the park is to chill out for a bit and catch his breath. Let's work on that." I looked down at Ollie, dancing and wheezing at my feet. "He *definitely* needs to take a break. The poor guy doesn't know when to quit!" I returned my gaze to Ollie. He shifted his weight from one side to the other and continued wheezing, his eyes at half-mast. "Ollie," he snapped to attention, not used to hearing me say his name. "Down."

He lowered himself into position, holding his head high. His breath was raspy. "Good boy! Stay." It was clear that he wasn't going anywhere. The guy was exhausted.

I turned back to Davis and Eileen. "Don't make him hold the stay for too long if you just arrived at the park. Because he's unleashed, he'll just take off before you release him, and there's nothing you can do about it. In this scenario," I pointed to Ollie, now drooling and panting at my feet, "there's little risk he's going to dash unless a dog comes right up to him. Watch him closely—he'll let you know when he's ready to go again."

Eileen offered Ollie a drink from a water bottle. His breathing pattern evened out, and he watched the dog pack moving from one side of the park to the other.

"Ollie, go play!" Davis exclaimed. Ollie popped up, revitalized, and raced toward his buddies.

"That was textbook perfect," I whooped, happy that Ollie was catching on to the game. We continued the process for fifteen more minutes. By the end of our visit, Ollie was checking in more often, and holding a quick down-stay without complaint. In fact, he looked relieved to be able to catch his breath!

We started walking toward the gate when it was finally time to leave. "Don't call him," I suggested. "Let's see if he checks in when we're close to the exit. Some dogs will hesitate to come close when they sense it's time to go. I have a feeling that won't be the case with Ollie, though."

"We usually do a recall, and he's *okay* about coming to us, but not great," Eileen said. "It takes a few repetitions, but he does come eventually."

"In a perfect world, he'll be so tuned in to the two of you and your whereabouts, he'll dash over for a check-in no matter where you are, even if you're standing by the dreaded exit," I explained. "And, there you go— he's on the way,'" I said, pointing to the happy, tongue-dragging dog racing toward us.

We praised wildly, Ollie basked, and Davis clipped the leash back on.

"Just to make sure he doesn't equate your position near the door with something to be avoided because he doesn't want to leave, stroll toward the door a few times during your visit, praise him when he checks in, and then send him out to play again. Once Ollie is checking in with you regularly, you can ease off on the cross-park trips."

I ran into Davis and Eileen a few weeks later and was happy to hear that Ollie had become a master at the get-lost game. "He checks in all the time, and he manages to hold the down-stay. Plus, it's not a struggle to get him to come along when it's time to go," Eileen reported.

The get-lost game is a simple way to shake up everyday life at the dog park and help your dog learn to keep an eye on you. The goal isn't slavish attention, though. A few simple check-ins or proximity-based acknowledgments that you're in the park, too, are enough to demonstrate your dog's interest in your whereabouts. The get-lost game might make you look antisocial to the other dog parents at the park, but your dog's increased attentiveness is a worthy trade-off!

One, Two, Three, Let's Go!

For some dogs, taking a walk is a chance to explore the open road. Finding out what's just over the next hill is their reason for being. "Onward and upward!" they seem to say. "No time to dawdle, let's walk, walk, walk!" For others, stopping to smell the roses is the main objective. And when I say "stopping," I mean it. They zero in on a patch of grass and inhale so deeply and with such focus that they seem to forget that they have a few more miles of sniffing available to them. The result is a staccato, stop-start walk that leaves both parties frustrated: your dog, because she keeps getting jerked along when she'd rather sniff a while longer, and you because you want to actually cover some ground during your walk.

Frustration doesn't make for good company during a leash walk. But you're in luck: There's an easy way to address super-sniffers that allows them to engage in the behavior without completely slowing the pace of the walk, or dragging them along as they try to get one last nose-full.

The next time your dog stops to breathe in a scent, allow her to do so instead of trying to pull her along with you. Pause for a few moments, and then give her a count: "One . . . two . . . three . . . let's go!" Once you hit the "let's go," begin walking. This is yet another teach-as-you-go cue, so the first time you try it, the cue will have no meaning—your dog will probably continue to sniff. When you resume walking, inertia will compel her to catch up to you, and when she does, even if it's reluctantly, give her a treat. Repeat the process the next time she finds an intriguing scent. The count gives her a clear signal that means "Finish up, we're about to keep going," instead of moving along without any warning.

I happen to live with the King of Sniffing. Zeke likes to pretend that he's a scent hound when we walk, which frustrates Sumner, who is an onward-and-upward kind of dog. Zeke is a strong little guy and will resist my efforts to move him along by lowering his heavy front end to the ground and digging in. I've employed the one-two-three technique with great success. Now he's often moving along after he hears me say "two."

This easy tweak to your walking routine is yet another way to reinforce the idea that a stroll is a collaborative effort, not a confrontation or test of wills. Allowing your dog her sniff time—but putting a cap on it—is a solution that works for both parties.

The one-two-three technique helps champion sniffers learn to move along promptly.

Wild, Wonderful

Bond-building and creativity go hand-in-hand. Doing something unusual, like pointing out a chipmunk hole for your dog to examine, might not seem like an obvious way to fast-track your relationship, but those quirky little moments add up. You might be surprised to discover how a few amazing discoveries and chased squirrels can help to move your bond in the right direction!

Chapter 10

BUILDING BLOCK #6: DON'T FORGET YOUR SENSE OF HUMOR

stood on the front step and paused a moment before I rang the doorbell. It was lesson three and I was dreading seeing Darcy and her husband James. It certainly wasn't because of their dog, Bonner, a sweet Wheaten Terrier puppy. I adored his nimble mind and willingness to learn. The problem in the household ran deeper than typical puppy problems, and I didn't have the qualifications to treat it. I heaved a sigh and rang the bell.

"She's here," I heard Darcy yelling as she headed to the front door. "Grab the dog, James. Grab him! Oh, come *on,* James, now he's right here at the front door with me. Thanks for your *help.*"

The commotion inside made my stomach twist. "An hour of this?" I thought to myself, heaving my eyes heavenward for no one's benefit but my own.

Darcy threw open the door with a sigh. "Hi. Rough morning in the Smith household," she smirked.

"Yeah, that doorbell stuff can be tough to deal with," I said, trying to make light of the turmoil unfolding before me as we walked through the entry hall. "Hey, did Bonner have an accident? What's with all the paper towels in the dining room?"

"I think you should talk to James about that. He's the one with all the answers."

Bonner greeted me with the enthusiasm I needed. James stood a few steps away in the kitchen, reading the newspaper. He barely glanced up at me as I entered the room.

"Good morning, James!" I trilled, making a point to be overly friendly.

"Hey," he replied. "Did she blame me for the accident in the dining room?"

"No, no blame. So what happened?"

James began a defensive, vitriol-filled review of the events that led up to Bonner's mess. Darcy interrupted him frequently, and the two raised their voices until I was embarrassed to be in the same room with them. The anger between them was palpable. I looked down at Bonner, who had his body pressed to my leg. I was immediately struck by how similar we must have appeared at that moment. The two of us sat silent and still, watching the drama play out. It was as if we were both trying to disappear into the toile couch. I turned my attention back to my bickering clients and suddenly felt very sorry for Bonner. "Oh, sweetie," I thought. "This is your life, you poor thing."

The rest of the lesson played out in a similar fashion. James and Darcy spat poison at each other while we worked on Bonner's down-stay. Listening to them made me cringe, but they barely even noticed my discomfort. Bonner kept his distance from them as well, but the weirdness in the room was lost on them.

Never once, in my entire six weeks with James and Darcy, did I laugh. In fact, I dreaded working with them. Keep in mind, we weren't addressing troubling puppy-related issues during our lessons. Bonner wasn't attacking their kids or shredding their antique quilts. I was there to help teach basic manners, which is normally an enjoyable, bond-building rite of passage for every new puppy. Bonner was the perfect student, and while any other household would have been thrilled with his efforts, James and Darcy only shrugged their shoulders at his achievements. I dissolved into giggles when Bonner consistently rolled onto his back and wiggled every time we asked for a down; James and Darcy remained unmoved. I cheered when Bonner nailed a challenging down-stay; James asked when Bonner would be able to do it without needing treats. There was no recognition of all that we were accomplishing, and no enjoyment in the process.

Though the problems in their household were out of my control, I was saddened that they couldn't rise above their unhappiness and enjoy their phenomenal, well-mannered puppy. I could tell that Bonner was suffering the effects of the joy-vacuum. He was a subdued dog not given to typical puppy goofiness, but that, too, was lost on them. Any puppy infraction—for example, a casual sniff in Darcy's briefcase or an inquisitive glance into the pantry—was met with a stern rebuke and a question of when he would "grow out of this phase."

James and Darcy's household remains the most dismal, unhappy scenario in my client roster. I often wonder how Bonner turned out, growing up in a home that seemed to lack any sense of fun. Did he manage to maintain his dog "spark," that innate sense of goofiness and humor that I love in dogs, or did his joyless environment force him to become a canine robot?

Laugh a Little

The single most important step in the bond building process is to enjoy the ride. Everything you do to grow your bond—from basic training to going on field trips to chasing squirrels—should be undertaken with a sense of humor. Your time with your dog is supposed to be *fun!* I leave many of my clients' homes with my cheeks aching from laughing and smiling so much, and I hope that my need to have a good time during training is contagious. I want my clients to feel that their training journey is something to be relished by both dog and human.

Your dog has a sense of humor—do you?

I always had a great time working with my clients Charlie, Matt, and their mini Australian Shepherd puppy, Rosie. Though they met me at the door each week with new tales of puppyhood woe ("She ate the homework you left for us" or "She went in the hamper and destroyed my socks") their frustration was tempered by their love for Rosie and their devilish senses of humor. During our lessons, they played off each other like a comedy team.

Their most impressive training feat (and funniest story) occurred about four weeks into our lessons. "Victoria, prepare to be amazed by what happened yesterday," Matt said, as I walked in the door.

"Oh no, " I replied. "Good or bad?"

"Well, really bad at first . . ." Matt began.

I braced myself. "Tell me."

"Our last dog, Olive, was awful with the UPS guy—"

"She bit him!" Charlie interrupted.

"So we wanted to make sure that the same thing didn't happen with Rosie because we have so many deliveries. We always give the UPS guy cookies to give to Rosie so she's happy to see him."

"And it's been working great," Charlie said. "He's totally her boyfriend now."

"Yeah, and that's the problem, Matt continued. "He showed up yesterday with our regular delivery and we propped open the door not realizing that Rosie was right there—"

Charlie interrupted again, "And she *took off!* She was out the door before we knew it, and she actually jumped *into* the UPS truck while the guy was in back getting our stuff!"

I looked at them with my jaw hanging open.

"No kidding," Matt continued, taking note of my speechlessness. "Luckily there weren't any cars coming. I tired to keep calm and said "Here!" in my happiest "I'm not angry—I promise" voice. Well, that little beggar started back to me immediately but stopped and looked up at the UPS guy, figured out in a split second that he didn't have a goodie for her yet, and then came tearing back into the house to wait for him!"

"That's awesome! I'm going to assume that all the recall training had something to do with her responsiveness when you called. . . ."

"Definitely," Charlie replied. "She nailed it. We were so relieved, and proud of her, too. We had the UPS guy give her cheese and had a little party because she did such a good job!"

They beamed at their dog while she danced in front of them. The happiness in Matt and Charlie's household was palpable. I adored working with them.

Although I wasn't able to shake James and Darcy from their pervasive unhappiness, I have been lucky enough to witness the halo effect of fun-focused dog training. I met with the Crandalls for the first time on a Thursday evening, and it was obvious that they were a family in flux. Gordon and his wife, Sandy, seemed at odds with each other, and their two preteens, Carter and Emily, had no desire to spend time with their parents and the goofy dog trainer. No one was happy. I struggled to keep the kids engaged during the introductory portion of the lesson, and keep Gordon and Sandy from overcorrecting their children and each other. Their dog, Spot? The excitement of being the center of attention for a change made him vibrate. He was a handful.

We started off with the basics, and, within minutes, we were all laughing at Spot's rabid enthusiasm for training. When he sat, it was with such speed and military precision that his rear thumped the floor each time. *Whomp!* He reacted with the same fervor for every member of the family, and I could see their reactions to Spot, and each other, changing as they worked with their dog. I sensed their shock that training Spot was actually enjoyable. I noticed Carter and Emily glancing furtively toward their parents each time they worked with the dog, looking for approval. I stepped up and praised them lavishly for their efforts, giggling with them each time Spot executed an Olympic-caliber sit. It didn't take long before Gordon and Sandy were joining me in the laughter and praise. The difference between the crossed-arm standoffishness I'd experienced when I first entered the house and what I was experiencing with them as we worked together thrilled me. It was clear that no one had been expecting to have a good time, and Spot had proved them wrong.

By the end of the first lesson, we'd covered basic sits, an introduction to down, and the recall. We had an easy camaraderie as we talked about homework. We grinned at our canine student splayed out on the floor in front of us. Kids talked to parents, parents talked to kids. "Mission accomplished," I thought to myself.

Gordon walked me out to the porch and placed his hand on my shoulder. "Can we hire you to do family therapy, too?" I laughed it off—it wasn't the first time I'd been asked that question. My private lessons allow me an insider's look at my clients' lives—the good and the bad—and I've been asked to kick in child psychology and marriage counseling as well. I was a little embarrassed that a simple dog-training lesson had highlighted the fun vacuum in Gordon's household but pleased that he was able to draw the parallel. We both knew that dog training wasn't going to "save" the family, but it gave them a reason to bond not only with their dog, but also with each other for a short time each week.

Frustration Is Inevitable

As you work your way through the bonding process, remember that it is a *process*. You're dealing with a living, breathing animal who has good days and bad days. Sometimes you'll wonder if your dog knows how to do anything, even a basic sit. That's *normal*—it happens. There's an ebb and flow to dog training and bond building, so don't be concerned when it seems like your dog has forgotten everything you've worked on. Setbacks are so common that I regularly warn my clients to expect the "week-three slump," which is when all previously learned dog skills seem to fall apart.

There will be times when your dog acts as if he doesn't understand a word you're saying, even after you've begun working on your bond.

Jingles the Bouvier puppy had been an exemplary canine client until late in the game: week five. Her person, Margaret, was agitated when I arrived for our lesson.

"I don't know what happened!" Margaret exclaimed to me. "She follows right behind me when I tell her to stay, she refuses to drop the ball when I ask, and she *urinated* on her bed when we were practicing! I tried to do our homework, but she was so bad this week."

"Let's think about Jingles's performance for us so far," I said, throwing my hands up to calm Margaret. "She's been beyond great, right? Picking up everything quickly, working joyfully in a bunch of distracting environments . . . she's been a dream student for me. Now we've hit a stumbling block. My only question is: What took her so long? Margaret, does your printer print perfectly every time? Does your cellphone connect every call you dial? Of course not, and those are *machines!* It's okay for Jingles to have a few off training sessions. Seriously. My only advice for you is to take it easy for a few days. Lay off the formal training sessions. Play with her, weave some training basics into your games, and try not to stress out. She hasn't forgotten our lessons, I promise. Let's see how she does today." Sure enough, Jingles was back to her old self by the end of the session.

It's easy to resort to the line, "He knows it—he's just being stubborn," when your dog refuses a simple cue. I caution my clients not to jump to the insubordination excuse when their dogs refuse to perform an exercise, though. Often, there are reasons a dog ignores a cue that have nothing to do with being disagreeable.

Every dog has off days, and that's okay!

Am I doing this right?

Feeling overwhelmed by information overload? A few simple questions can help you determine if you're headed in the right direction with Fido:

- **Is your dog having a good time?** This question separates the old-school be-the-alpha approach to living and working with a dog from modern dog-friendly training. **Remember:** drills are for the military and the tool chest. Your dog will learn more and retain more if you keep your training sessions fun.

- **Are you having a good time?** You're more likely to stick with the program if you're actually enjoying it.

- **Are you comfortable with the methods you're using?** Gut check: Does it feel right? If kneeing Fido in the chest because he's jumping doesn't sit well with you, *don't do it.*

Most of the dogs I work with initially refuse to assume the down position on a hard floor (it's a safe assumption that it's uncomfortable), so we work on a carpeted patch until the dog fully understands the cue. Young wiggly puppies have a hard time maintaining a sit-stay on slick floors, so I never ask them to unless they have some traction like an area rug. Some dogs feel nervous working in certain areas of the house—because of a loud fan, for example. Some feel strange about working near doorways. Some have baggage about approaching on a recall because of past scolding. If your dog is consistently refusing a cue, look deeper for the possible hidden reasons why before you affix an undeserving label like "stubborn."

You will get frustrated as you work on your bond. You'll have many, many off days. Plan on some all-out bad days as well. Bond building is not a linear procedure, but one of fits and starts. Before you give up on your dog, take a step back and recognize *any* progress he's made. (We're so programmed to look only for major successes that the little ones are often forgotten.) One amazing recall out of three? That's a start! Dropping the empty potato-chip bag when you asked? Fantastic! Keeping an eye on you while at the dog park? Now that's progress.

It's Not Rocket Science

It's easy to be flummoxed by the information overload that is dog training. Everyone has an opinion about how it should be done, and everyone is

Enjoy every step of your bond-building journey.

convinced that their way is the right way. (My way is the right way, of course.) Couple that fire hose of information with your desire to just do it right and you're guaranteed to feel the enjoyment of working with your dog slipping away. Though I've given you a long list of tips and techniques for strengthening your relationship with your dog, the core of my bond-building process rests in two words: Have fun. If you enjoy the journey, the destination will come that much faster.

INDEX

ABOUT VICTORIA SCHADE

VICTORIA SCHADE is an award-winning, APDT-certified Pet Dog Trainer, author, and television host located in Washington, D.C. Since founding her company, Good Dog! Obedience Training, eight years ago, Victoria has worked with thousands of dogs and owners to hone her unique dog handling and coaching technique, winning her a "Best Trainer" award from *Washingtonian* magazine two years in a row. An honors graduate from the San Francisco SPCA Academy for Dog Trainers with a Counseling Certificate, she has earned rave reviews for her ability to help every dog be a good dog by using an approach of mutual love, trust, and respect.

Victoria is currently a host for Animal Planet's *Faithful Friends,* a program that gives insight and advice for taking care of a variety of pets. Her gentle, engaging style has led to regular television appearances, including CBS's *The Early Show,* WE tv, WJLA-ABC News Channel 7, and WTTG Fox Channel 5, and inspired the creation of her award-winning puppy-training DVD, *New Puppy! Now What?,* a lighthearted take on the

trials of raising a happy, healthy puppy. She's helped cast and coach three consecutive *Puppy Bowl* TV shows on Animal Planet, as well as the channel's
Olympic-themed special *The Puppy Games.* Victoria also recently trained and
coached the dogs for the Smithsonian Channel special, *Animals Aloft.*

Victoria frequently serves as a resource for the media on topics related to
dog handling and puppy training, and has been quoted in outlets such as *The
Washington Post, The Washington Times, The (D.C.) Examiner, Washingtonian,
Northern Virginia Living, Dog Fancy, The Bark, Dogs USA,* as well as the
Training Secrets magazines (German Shepherds, Boxers, and Labradors).

For more information, visit www.gooddogobedience.com, and check out
Victoria's blog, www.lifeontheleash.com.